FESTIVE
COCKTAILS
& canapés

Festive Cocktails
& canapés

over **100** recipes for seasonal drinks
and party bites

with photography by
ALEX LUCK

RYLAND PETERS & SMALL
LONDON • NEW YORK

Senior Designer Toni Kay
Editorial Director Julia Charles
Creative Director Leslie Harrington
Production Manager Gordana Simakovic
Indexer Vanessa Bird

First published in 2022
by Ryland Peters & Small,
20–21 Jockey's Fields,
London WC1R 4BW
and
341 E 116th St,
New York NY 10029

www.rylandpeters.com

10 9 8 7 6 5 4 3 2 1

Recipe collection compiled by Julia Charles.
Recipes © copyright Julia Charles, Jesse Estes, Lydia
France, Laura Gladwin, Hannah Miles, Ben Reed,
David T. Smith & Keli Rivers 2022. Design and photographs
© Ryland Peters & Small 2022. See page 160 for full text
and picture credits.

ISBN: 978-1-78879-480-0

A CIP record for this book is available from
the British Library.

US Library of Congress cataloging-in-publication data
has been applied for.

Printed and bound in China.

NOTES

• Both metric (ml), imperial (oz.) and US cups are
included for your convenience. Work with one set of
measurements and do not alternate between the
two within a recipe.

• When a recipe calls for citrus zest or peel, buy
unwaxed fruit and wash well before using. If you
can only find treated fruit, scrub well in warm
soapy water before using.

• To sterilize screw-top jars and bottles to store
homemade cocktail syrups, preheat the oven to
160°C/150°C fan/325°F/ Gas 3. Wash the jars and/or bottles
and their lids in hot soapy water then rinse but don't
dry them. Remove any rubber seals, put the jars onto
a baking sheet and into the oven for 10 minutes. Soak
the lids in boiling water for a few minutes.

• Popaball® 'Bursting Bubbles' are used in the cocktail
on page 98, however, their inclusion in recipes is optional.
Visit www.popaball.co.uk for more information about
the product.

MIX
Paper | Supporting
responsible forestry
FSC® C008047

CONTENTS

INTRODUCTION

Christmas is indeed the most wonderful time of the year. The holiday season arrives, bringing with it invitations to a host of events from large cocktail parties to intimate celebratory dinners with family and loved ones. It seems social occasions quickly fill up our diaries and when your turn to host a gathering inevitably arrives, it can be stressful, especially at a time of year when time to plan and shop is in short supply. As your family and friends come together to eat drink and be merry at your home, let this collection of drinks and canapés see you through – from advent to New Year's Eve. You'll find everything you need to create truly memorable social occasions with recipes for classic cocktails, sparkling aperitifs, dessert cocktails and fun party drinks, as well as delicious small bites and canapés, you will be well equip to cater for every type of occasion.

Stylish cocktails that can be rustled up from a well-stocked festive bar cart include a a Mini Martini, New York Sour, Bramble and White Manhattan. When it's time to break out the bubbly, take your presentation up a notch with sparkling cocktails, such as a Blackberry Bellini, Chambles or Prosecco Classico. Tangy aperitifs designed to whet your guests' appetites, include a Chelsea Sidecar, French 75 and Zaza. Party drinks should always be colourful and fun so take your pick from a Clementine Caipirinha, Singapore Sling or Rose & Pomegranate Cosmo. Decadent dessert cocktails and nightcaps are making a comeback, so why not end the evening sipping on a Chocatini, Espresso Martini or Snowgroni (a fun Negroni-inspired twist on a Snowball)? The methods for all the drinks are easy to follow and require little or no specialist equipment, though any home bartender can always use a cocktail shaker, a measuring jigger and a few pieces of classic glassware, such as old-fashioned, coupe and martini glasses, but often a small wine glass or tumbler will work just as well. Champagne flutes and wine glasses are always available to hire, so do plan ahead and rent what you need for any larger events. Punch bowls make a wonderful focal point on any festive party table, from simple glass to cut crystal, so if you are lucky enough to have one, possibly even a family heirloom, now is the season to get it out and show it off! If not, any large bowl or jug/pitcher can be used.

For the ultimate in hospitality, offer a selection of delicious homemade canapés with your well-made drinks. The savoury and sweet recipes here are designed to take the stress out of finding the perfect bite to accompany your tipples and satisfy hungry guests. They range from simple no-cook ideas to those that need a little preparation or cooking, but they will knock the (cosy) socks off of anything you can buy ready-made, and suggestions as to what works well together are included. Add pizzazz to your festive event with melt-in-the-mouth nibbles such as Cheese Straws and Anchovy Wafers, both perfect with chilled Champagne; or larger bites, such as Slow Roasted Tomato Galettes with Black Olive Tapenade & Goats' Cheese, Parsnip & Apple Remoulade with Bayonne Ham on Rye, Smoked Salmon Mousse Croustades or Caesar Salad Tartlets. Bite-size sweet treats to end the evening include Snowy Pine Nut Cookies, Apple & Calvados Pies and Salted Chocolate-dipped Figs, all delicious served with a warm glass of Swedish Glögg. You'll find all you need here to guarantee plenty of festive cheer and get your guests into the Christmas spirit - *Happy Holidays!*

We hope you enjoy this festive recipe collection and discover new drinks that bring you comfort and joy and fill your home with good cheer this winter.

Bar cart
classics

MINI MARTINIS

Here a timeless classic is scaled down and served in a minature cocktail glass to make the perfect aperitif, add a stuffed olive to garnish, or serve with a Green Olive & Anchovy Tapenade Crostini (recipe page 136).

15 ml/$^{1}/_{2}$ oz. Noilly Prat,
   or other dry vermouth
75 ml/3 oz. London dry gin
   (such as Beefeater)
2 stuffed green olives, to garnish
   (optional, see recipe intro)

SERVES 2

Pour the vermouth and gin over cracked ice in a glass or metal mixing jug/pitcher. Stir to make the cocktail very cold. Strain into 2 small chilled cocktail glasses. Garnish with an olive, if using, and serve at once.

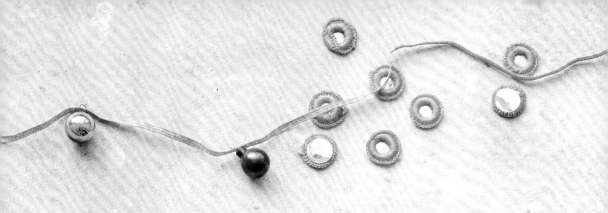

Boulevardier

This variation on a Negroni is thought to have been invented by Erskine Gwynne, an American writer who lived in Paris and was a regular at Harry MacElhone's bar in that great city. The drink shared its name with the monthly magazine that Gwynne edited, 'The Boulevardier'.

25 ml/1 oz. Maker's Mark Bourbon
25 ml/1 oz. Cocchi Vermouth di Torino, or other red vermouth
25 ml/1 oz. Campari
an orange zest, to garnish

SERVES 1

Add all the ingredients to an ice-filled mixing glass and stir vigorously. Strain into a coupe glass, garnish with a piece of orange peel and serve at once.

Old Pal

A lighter and less sweet version of The Boulevardier (see above).

25 ml/1 oz. rye whiskey
25 ml/1 oz. Cocchi Americano
25 ml/1 oz. Campari
a lemon zest, to garnish

SERVES 1

Add the ingredients to an ice-filled mixing glass and stir vigorously. Strain into a rocks glass (with ice if liked), garnish with a lemon spiral and serve at once.

New York sour

*A red wine float provides a delectably festive twist
on the classic whiskey sour.*

50 ml/1²/₃ oz. Bulleit Bourbon
25 ml/³/₄ oz. fresh lemon juice
25 ml/³/₄ oz. sugar syrup
1 dash of Angostura bitters
20 ml/²/₃ oz. egg white
25 ml/³/₄ oz. red wine
an edible flower, to garnish

SERVES 1

Combine all the drink ingredients, except the wine, in a
cocktail shaker and 'dry' shake without ice to emulsify the
egg white. Add a scoop of cubed ice, then shake hard and
strain into a small wine glass over cubed ice. Pour the red
wine slowly over the back of a bar spoon or teaspoon to
'float' a layer of red wine over the cocktail. Garnish with
an edible flower and serve at once.

Ward eight

*Named after a voting district in Boston once famous for its political
corruption, the ward eight is a somewhat forgotten classic cocktail
that shows how well rye whiskey can pair with orange juice.*

50 ml/1²/₃ oz. Michter's
    Straight Rye Whiskey
25 ml/³/₄ oz. fresh lemon juice
25 ml/³/₄ oz. fresh orange juice
7.5 ml/1½ teaspoons grenadine
10 ml/2 teaspoons sugar syrup
    (or to taste)
an orange wedge and Luxardo
    maraschino cherry, to garnish

SERVES 1

Add all the drink ingredients to a cocktail shaker
with a scoop of cubed ice and shake hard. Strain into
a chilled coupe glass, garnish with an orange wedge
and a cherry and serve at once.

BRAMBLE

A drink for gin lovers. (Pictured with Beef with Blackberry Sauce & Watercress Toasts, recipe page 139.)

50 ml/2 oz. London dry gin
25 ml/¾ oz. lemon juice
10 ml/2 teaspoons sugar syrup
15 ml/1 tablespoon Crème de Mûre
   (blackberry liqueur)
a lemon slice and a fresh
   blackberry, to garnish

SERVES 2

Add some crushed ice to each of the serving glasses. Shake the gin, lemon juice and sugar syrup in an ice-filled cocktail shaker and strain into the prepared glasses. Drizzle half of the Crème de Mûre over the top of each drink so that it bleeds into the pale mixture. (Do not stir.) Garnish with a lemon slice and a blackberry and serve at once.

Sweet Manhattan

Perhaps one of the most iconic cocktails of all time, there is a reason that the manhattan is a tried-and-true classic. Bourbon pairs beautifully with sweet vermouth and bitters: together they are a match made in heaven. The manhattan is also the basis for countless variations – for instance substitute bourbon for Scotch and you've got a Rob Roy.

50 ml/²⁄₃ oz. Jefferson's Reserve
   Bourbon, or similar
25 ml/³⁄₄ oz. Cocchi Vermouth
   di Torino, or other sweet
   vermouth
3 dashes of Angostura bitters
an orange zest
a Luxardo maraschino cherry,
   to garnish

SERVES 1

Combine all the drink ingredients in a mixing glass with a scoop of cubed ice. Stir for about 30 seconds before straining into a chilled coupette glass. Squeeze the orange zest to express the citrus oils over the drink and discard. Garnish with a Luxardo maraschino cherry and serve at once.

Old Fashioned

If you enjoy Bourbon in a cocktail it doesn't get any better than a well-made Old Fashioned. (Pictured page 108.)

1 white sugar cube
2 dashes of Angostura bitters
50 ml/2 oz. bourbon or
   rye whiskey
an orange zest, to garnish

SERVES 1

Put a sugar cube in a rocks glass. Splash with the bitters until the cube is saturated. Muddle until crushed and syrupy, adding just a little water if necessary to achieve this. Pour in the bourbon and add ice. Stir and then twist the orange zest on the surface of the drink just to release the orange oils and drop it into the glass. Serve at once.

White Manhattan

Unaged American whiskey (nicknamed 'white dog') has gained cult status in recent years. This drink uses it and other 'white' ingredients for a variation on the manhattan that is ideal for the holiday season.

40 ml/1⅓ oz. Georgia Moon
   Corn Whiskey
20 ml/⅔ oz. Cocchi Americano
3 dashes of white wine vinegar
10 ml/2 teaspoons Suze (bitters
   flavoured with gentian root)
1 dash of orange bitters
a lemon zest, to garnish

SERVES 1

Stir all the drink ingredients together in a mixing glass with a scoop of cubed ice for around 20–30 seconds. Strain into a chilled coupe glass. Squeeze the lemon zest to express the citrus oils over the top and sides of the drink and use to garnish the glass. Serve at once.

Vieux Carré

Pronounced 'voo ka-ray', the name of this drink translates to 'old square', the French term for New Orleans' French Quarter.

30 ml/1 oz. Sazerac
   Rye Whiskey
30 ml/1 oz. Cognac
30 ml/1 oz. Martini Rosso,
   or other sweet vermouth
7.5 ml/1½ teaspoons Benedictine
1 dash of Angostura bitters
1 dash of Peychaud's bitters
a large lemon zest, to garnish

SERVES 1

Stir all the drink ingredients together in a mixing glass with a scoop of cubed ice for around 15–20 seconds. Strain into a rocks glass over cubed ice. Squeeze the lemon zest to express the citrus oils over the top and sides of the drink and use to garnish the glass. Serve at once.

BEE'S KNEES

A still-popular Prohibition era cocktail. (Pictured opposite with Endive Cups with Roquefort Mousse, recipe page 126.)

25 ml/1 oz. lemon juice
20 ml/³/₄ oz. honey syrup (see below)
50 ml/2 oz. London dry gin, preferably Beefeater

HONEY SYRUP
140 g/¹/₂ cup runny acacia honey
40 ml/¹/₆ cup hot water

SERVES 1

First make the honey syrup. Combine the honey and hot water in a heatproof bowl and stir until completely mixed.

Half-fill a cocktail shaker with ice and add the lemon juice, honey syrup and gin. Shake vigorously for 7 seconds until chilled and strain into a coupe glass. Serve at once.

AVIATION

This beautiful violet cocktail dates from the early 1900s and is always a conversation starter!

50 ml/2 oz. gin
5 ml/1 teaspoon Luxardo Maraschino liqueur
5 ml/1 teaspoon crème de violette
25 ml/1 oz. lemon juice
a Luxardo maraschino cherry, to garnish

SERVES 1

Add all the ingredients to a cocktail shaker full of ice. Shake until frosted. Strain into a cocktail glass or small coupe and garnish with a single maraschino cherry and serve at once.

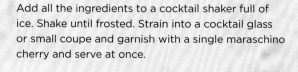

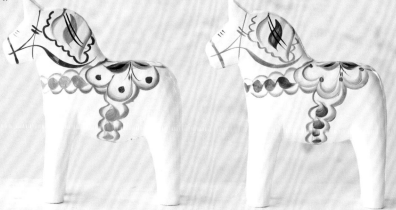

Bobby Burns

This twist on the Rob Roy (see page 18) was named after Scottish poet Robert Burns. To add extra depth to the drink, try including a dash of absinthe and/or orange bitters. The smokiness of the Scotch works perfectly with the herbaceous and spicy notes of the Benedictine.

50 ml/1²/₃ oz. Glenmorangie
The Original Single Malt
Scotch Whisky
25 ml/³/₄ oz. Martini Rosso,
or other sweet vermouth
12.5 ml/2¹/₂ teaspoons Benedictine
a lemon zest, to garnish

SERVES 1

Combine all the drink ingredients in a mixing glass with a scoop of cubed ice. Stir for about 30 seconds before straining into a chilled coupette glass. Squeeze the lemon zest to express the citrus oils over the drink before using to garnish the glass. Serve at once.

Rusty Nail

This blend of Drambuie (a honeyed, herbed and spiced whiskey liqueur) and Scotch was huge in the 60s and doesn't disappoint today. (Pictured page 114.)

45 ml/1¹/₂ oz. Scotch whiskey
25 ml/³/₄ oz. Drambuie

SERVES 1

Fill a rocks or old-fashioned glass with ice cubes. Add the whiskey and Drambuie and stir to chill. Serve at once. (Alternatively, you can serve the drink without ice in a small stemmed glass, as pictured left.)

Kingston Negroni

This is a rum-based version of a Negroni that marries the herbal complexity of the cocktail with the warm, intense and gently sweet character of rum. The drink works with a variety of rums, but the best results come from using a Jamaican pot-still rum such as Smith & Cross, which is packed full of complex spicy flavours, and helps to make the perfect warming drink for the colder months.

25 ml/1 oz. Smith & Cross
   Jamaican Rum
25 ml/1 oz. red vermouth
25 ml/1 oz. Campari
a flamed orange zest, to garnish

SERVES 1

Add the ingredients to an ice-filled mixing glass and stir. Strain into an ice-filled rocks glass. Finish and garnish with a flamed orange twist and serve at once.

Variation For a less intense drink, mix 30 ml/1 oz. Cachaça (a Brazilian cane spirit) or white rum with 30 ml/1 oz. bianco vermouth, 15 ml/$\frac{1}{2}$ oz. Campari, and 15 ml/$\frac{1}{2}$ oz. lime juice. Shake in an ice-filled cocktail shaker and pour (without straining) the entire contents of the shaker into a rocks glass. Add more ice and garnish with a lime wedge. Serve at once.

Sparklers & Aperitifs

Sparkling Manhattan

If you love Manhattans, you'll love this. This is based on a Sweet Manhattan (see page 18), but switch the sweet vermouth for dry if you prefer yours dry, or use half sweet and half dry vermouth if you're more of a Perfect Manhattan fan.

15 ml/½ oz. bourbon
10 ml/⅓ oz. sweet red vermouth
1 dash of Angostura bitters
5 ml/1 teaspoon Luxardo Maraschino Liqueur
well-chilled Champagne or other dry
    sparkling wine, to top up
3 Luxardo maraschino cherries, to garnish

SERVES 1

Pour the first four ingredients into an ice-filled cocktail shaker and stir well.

Strain into a chilled old-fashioned glass and top up with Champagne.

Garnish with maraschino cherries and serve at once.

Santa's Little Helper

Forget the milk and gingerbread cookies – this is what Santa really wants to find when he calls at your home this holiday season.

20 ml/¾ oz. Pedro Ximenez sherry
15 ml/½ oz. ginger wine
15 ml/½ oz. freshly squeezed
    orange juice
well-chilled Prosecco, to top up
a strip of orange zest, to garnish

SERVES 1

Put the sherry, ginger wine and orange juice in a cocktail shaker and add a handful of ice cubes. Shake well and strain into a chilled Champagne flute. Top up with Prosecco. Squeeze the orange zest strip in half lengthways so that the essential oils in the skin spritz on to the drink, then drop it in. Serve at once.

CRANBERRY CASSIS

This slightly dryer and fruitier twist on a Kir Royale would be perfect for a festive brunch gathering. The cranberry adds a little special Christmas magic, but it's refreshing and light at any time of year.

35 ml/1½ oz. cranberry juice
15 ml/½ oz. crème de cassis
well-chilled Prosecco or other
 dry sparkling wine, to top up
a sprig of redcurrants, to garnish
 (optional)

SERVES 1

Pour the first two ingredients into an ice-filled cocktail shaker and shake well.

 Strain into a chilled Champagne flute or small wine glass and top up with Prosecco. Garnish with redcurrants, if liked, and serve at once.

MIMOSA

Presenting the Bucks Fizz's chic cousin from across the pond: the Mimosa, which is beautifully enhanced by a dash of Cointreau.

about 65 ml/2¾ oz. well-chilled
 freshly squeezed orange juice
5 ml/1 teaspoon Cointreau
well-chilled Prosecco or other dry
 sparkling wine, to top up

SERVES 1

Half-fill a cold Champagne flute with the orange juice. Add the Cointreau and half the Prosecco. Stir gently, then add the rest and serve at once.

Note: If you're making a trayful, help the bubbles stay perky by adding half the Prosecco and stirring all the glasses. Finish off with the final dose of Prosecco just before serving.

CRANBERRY & ORANGE SPARKLER

This is the ideal companion to a festive breakfast or brunch. It's light, refreshing and if you use an Italian Vino Frizzante, it will be a little lower in alcohol than a Prosecco or Champagne-based cocktail, so perfect for drinking before midday!

10 ml/¼ oz. Cointreau or other orange-flavoured liqueur
40 ml/1½ oz. cranberry juice, well chilled
80–100 ml/2½–3⅓ oz. lightly sparkling rosé wine, such as an Italian Rosato Vino Frizzante
an orange zest and/or fresh cranberries, to garnish

SERVES 1

Pour the Cointreau and cranberry juice into a Champagne flute and top up with cold sparkling rosé wine. Garnish with a twist of orange zest and/or a few fresh cranberries on a cocktail stick, if liked. Serve at once.

BLACKBERRY BELLINI

A classic Venetian bellini is white peach purée paired with Prosecco but the sour-sweetness of ripe blackberries works beautifully here to create a winter-time variation.

4 fresh blackberries, plus 1 extra, to garnish
1 teaspoon white caster/superfine sugar
30 ml/1 oz. vodka
10 ml/2 teaspoons lemon juice
well-chilled rosé Prosecco, to top up

SERVES 1

Put the 4 blackberries and sugar in a cocktail shaker and gently muddle with a muddler or handle of a rolling pin.

Add the ice cubes, vodka and lemon juice to the shaker and shake until cold, about 20 seconds. Strain into a Champagne flute, top up with cold rosé Prosecco and garnish with a blackberry on a cocktail stick. Serve at once.

Lavender French 75

This floral twist to a classic French 75 (see page 53) adds just a hint of perfume, barely there but enough to transport you to the lavender fields of Provence.

(Pictured with Goats' Cheese & Pink Peppercorn Balls, recipe page 129.)

50 ml/2 oz. gin
30 ml/1 oz. freshly squeezed
    lemon juice
20 ml/$\frac{1}{2}$ oz. Monin lavender syrup
ice cubes, to shake
well-chilled Champagne or
    Crémant, to top up
lemon twists, to garnish

SERVES 2

Pour the gin, lemon juice and lavender syrup into a cocktail shaker filled with ice cubes. Shake until frosted then strain the mixture into a small jug/pitcher and divide between 2 flutes.

Carefully top up with well-chilled Champagne or Crémant and garnish each with a lemon twist. Serve at once.

Zaza

Named after an 1898 French play that was made into a film several times – a rags-to-riches tale of a music-hall entertainer who becomes the mistress of an aristocrat – the darkly glamorous Zaza will add a little drama to any gathering. (Pictured page 44.)

35 ml/1½ oz. gin
35 ml/1½ oz. Dubonnet
1 dash of Angostura bitters
a Luxardo maraschino cherry
    or orange zest, to garnish

SERVES 1

Fill a cocktail shaker with ice cubes and add the gin, Dubonnet and bitters. Stir well and strain into a chilled cocktail glass. Garnish with a maraschino cherry or twist of orange zest and serve at once.

Kir Reali

The French have their Kir Royale (sparkling wine with crème de cassis), and the Kir Reali is the Italian version. It's a great way to elevate a glass of Prosecco for a special occasion.

10 ml/⅓ oz. crème de violette
125 ml/4½ oz. well-chilled
    Prosecco
a strip of lemon zest, to garnish

SERVES 1

Pour the crème de violette into a chilled Champagne flute and add the Prosecco. Squeeze the lemon zest in half lengthways over the drink so that the essential oils in the skin spritz over it, then drop it in and serve at once.

KIR BLUSH

A kir is a staple of the Parisian café scene. This variation pairs a fruity rosé with softer raspberry crème de framboise for a perfectly pink aperitif. (Pictured page 45, front.)

30 ml/1 oz. crème de framboise
about 125 ml/½ cup dry but fruity
 rosé wine, well chilled, such as
 a French rosé from the Rhône
 or Bordeaux works

SERVES 1

Pour the crème de framboise into the base of a white wine glass, then top up with cold rosé wine. Serve at once.

CHAMBLES

The decadent black raspberry liqueur Chambord adds extra fruitiness with just a hint of creamy vanilla to a glass of sparkling rosé. (Pictured page 45, back.)

30 ml/1 oz. Chambord
about 125 ml/½ cup sparkling rosé
 wine, well chilled, such as
 a dry rosé Crémant or
 pink Champagne
a fresh raspberry, to garnish

SERVES 1

Pour the Chambord into the base of a tall flute, then top up with cold sparkling rosé wine. Garnish with a fresh raspberry. Serve at once.

PROSECCO CLASSICO

If it's good enough for Champagne, it's good enough for Prosecco! Roll out the red carpet and give yours the Hollywood star treatment by serving it in classic sparkling cocktail style.

a few dashes of Angostura bitters
1 brown sugar cube
a dash of brandy
125 ml/4¹/₂ oz. well-chilled Prosecco

SERVES 1

Drop several dashes of Angostura bitters onto the sugar cube and put it in a chilled Champagne flute. Add a dash of brandy, then add the Prosecco and serve at once.

PROSECCO WHITE LADY

A cocktail legend made even lovelier, thanks to a generous helping of Prosecco. The White Lady is a slinky, sophisticated 1920s classic – and so will you be once you've sipped one of these!

35 ml/1¹/₂ oz. gin
15 ml/¹/₂ oz Cointreau
well-chilled Prosecco, to top up
15 ml/¹/₂ oz lemon juice

SERVES 1

Pour the gin and Cointreau into a cocktail shaker half-filled with ice cubes. Stir until very cold, then strain into a chilled martini glass. Top up with Prosecco and the lemon juice and serve at once.

Vanilla White Lady

This twist on the White Lady gin and cointreau cocktail makes
a 'snowy' Christmas party aperitif. (Pictured opposite with Parsnip
& Apple Remoulade with Bayonne Ham on Rye, recipe page 117.)

50 ml/2 oz. gin
15 ml/¹/₂ oz. lemon juice
15 ml/¹/₂ oz. Cointreau
¹/₂ a vanilla pod/bean
white caster/superfine sugar,
   to rim the glasses (optional)

SERVES 2

Rim the glasses with sugar, if using.
   Place the gin, lemon juice, Cointreau and vanilla
pod/bean in a cocktail shaker with a few ice cubes.
Shake well until frosted, remove the vanilla pod/bean
and pour into the sugar-rimmed serving glasses.
Serve at once.

Chelsea Sidecar

Replace Cognac in a classic Sidecar cocktail with gin, and this is
what you get. Deliciously tart and crisp and perfect to make in
a batch. (Pictured page 118.)

45 ml/1¹/₂ oz. dry gin
30 ml/1 oz. triple sec
30 ml/1 oz. lemon juice
5 ml/1 teaspoon sugar syrup
lemon twist, to garnish

SERVES 1

Shake all the ingredients in an ice-filled cocktail
shaker and strain into a chilled martini glass.
Garnish with a lemon twist and serve at once.

APPLEBLACK

The perfect choice for a sophisticated drinks party, the Appleblack offers a more potent alternative to the Kir Royale. Its apple and blackcurrant flavours make it ideal for winter gatherings.

15 ml/½ oz. Calvados
15 ml/½ oz crème de cassis
well-chilled crémant de Loire,
  or other dry sparkling wine,
  to top up

SERVES 1

Pour the Calvados and crème de cassis into an ice-filled cocktail shaker and stir well. Strain into a chilled Champagne flute, top up with crémant de Loire and serve at once.

FRENCH 75

The epitome of elegance, a French 75 is the perfect aperitif for almost any occasion. Gin, Champagne, lemon juice and sugar syrup – so simple but so effective. (See page 41 for a floral variation.)

35 ml/1¼ oz. gin
10 ml/2 teaspoons lemon juice
   (pulp removed)
5 ml/1 teaspoon sugar syrup
chilled Champagne, to top up

SERVES 1

Add the gin, lemon juice and sugar syrup to a cocktail shaker. Add ice cubes, shake until chilled and strain into a flute glass. Top up with chilled Champagne and serve at once.

Note: To cater for a party multiply the ingredients by the number of servings you need and premix a batch of the gin, lemon and sugar then pop it in the fridge for 1–2 hours. This means that no ice is needed. Once cold, measure 50 ml/2 oz. of the premix into the glass, top up with chilled Champagne and serve at once.

BELLO MARCELLO

Even the most committed whisky-phobe will love this lighter,
spritzed way of enjoying it. (Pictured page 56.)

35 ml/1½ oz. whisky
15 ml/½ oz. Cointreau
well-chilled Prosecco, to top up
a strip of lemon zest, to garnish

SERVES 1

Pour the whisky and Cointreau into an old-fashioned
glass filled with ice. Stir well, then top up with Prosecco.
Squeeze the lemon zest in half lengthways over the
drink so that the essential oils in the skin spritz over it,
then serve at once.

BRIDGE OF SIGHS

This was named after the enclosed bridge in Venice and your guests will surely sigh with delight after one sip of this sparkler. Sugar-frosting the rim of the glass adds a nice decorative touch. (Pictured page 57.)

caster/superfine sugar, to decorate
   the glass (optional)
15 ml/$\frac{1}{2}$ oz. gin
15 ml/$\frac{1}{2}$ oz. elderflower liqueur
well-chilled Prosecco, to top up

SERVES 1

If you like, moisten the rim of a chilled Champagne flute with water and dip it into a saucer filled with caster/superfine sugar to create a rim around the glass.

Put the gin and elderflower liqueur in a cocktail shaker with a handful of ice cubes and stir. Strain carefully into the flute. Add half the Prosecco and stir gently, then add the rest and serve at once.

PARTY
DRINKS

CLEMENTINE CAIPIRINHA

A Caipirinha is made by 'muddling' lime wedges with sugar in a glass to extract all their juice. Crushed iced then goes in, followed by a measure of cachaça. Using clementines in place of limes brings a festive twist. (Pictured opposite with Brie & Cranberry Sauce Puffs, recipe page 132).

1 whole clementine
1 fresh lime, cut into wedges
2 teaspoons demerara/turbinado
    sugar
60 ml/2 oz. cachaça
    (Brazilian sugar cane spirit)

SERVES 1

Remove the ends from the clementine and slice it into quarters, being sure to remove any of the white pith in the centre of the segments.

Put into a cocktail shaker with a lime wedge and sugar and pound with a muddler or end of a wooden rolling pin to extract the juice. Add the cachaça with plenty of ice cubes and shake well.

Strain into a small crushed-ice filled tumbler and serve with a short straw. Garnish with lime wedges, if liked, and serve at once.

SNAP APPLE

The light and fresh flavours of Scandinavia come together here to make a refreshingly sparkling shot. (Pictured page 117.)

30 ml/1 oz. aquavit
30 ml/1 oz. green (sour)
    apple liqueur
a squeeze of lime juice
a few dashes of sparkling clear
    lemonade
green apple slices, to garnish

SERVES 2

Half-fill a cocktail shaker with ice. Add the aquavit, apple liqueur and a squeeze of lime juice. Shake until frosted then pour into shot glasses.

Add an apple slice to each serving and top up with chilled sparkling lemonade. Serve at once.

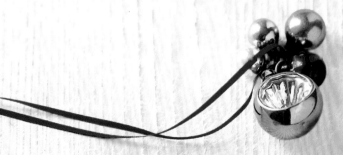

HAVANA NIGHTS

In 1950s Havana, Ernest Hemingway used to drink his daiquiris at El Floridita and his mojitos at La Bodeguita. Now you can have the best of both worlds with this delicious sparkling party version!

8 mint leaves
5 ml/1 teaspoon sugar syrup
10 ml/^{1}/$_5$ oz. lime juice
25 ml/1 oz. aged (dark) rum
well-chilled Prosecco or other
   dry sparkling wine, to top up
lime zest or slice, to garnish
   (optional)

SERVES 1

Muddle the mint leaves with the sugar syrup in a cocktail shaker. Add the lime juice and rum with a handful of ice cubes and shake well.

   Strain into a chilled flute and top up with Prosecco. Garnish with lime, if you like, and serve at once.

LA PALOMA

Sour, sweet and salty, La Paloma gives the Margarita (see page 71) a run for it's money in Mexico. (Pictured page 120.)

60 ml/2 oz. silver tequila
30 ml/1 oz. pink grapefruit juice
15 ml/^{1}/$_2$ oz. lime juice
7.5 ml/^{1}/$_2$ tablespoon agave syrup
pink grapefruit soda or tonic
   water, to top up
pink sea salt, for rimming
   the glasses
pink grapefruit wedges, to garnish
   (optional)

SERVES 1

First prepare the glass. Spread out some pink sea salt on a small saucer and add a little water to another. Dip the rim of the glass first into the water, then into the salt. Set aside.

   Pour the tequila, grapefruit juice, lime juice and agave syrup into an ice-filled cocktail shaker and shake until frosted. Strain into the salt-rimmed glass and serve at once.

Singapore Sling

This fruity gin-based cocktail is said to have been invented at Raffles Hotel, Singapore in 1915 so has earned the right to be called a classic. (Pictured page 84 with Cheese & Spicy Roasted Pineapple Sticks, recipe page 145.)

45 ml/1½ oz. gin
10 ml/2 teaspoons cherry brandy
5 ml/1 teaspoon Benedictine
5 ml/1 teaspoon Triple Sec
15 ml/1 tablespoon pineapple juice
30 ml/1 oz. lemon juice
2 dashes of Angostura bitters
soda water/club soda, to top up
lemon zests and cocktail cherries,
    to garnish

SERVES 1

Pour all the ingredients into a small jug/pitcher filled with ice and stir gently to mix.

Pour into ice-filled serving glasses, top up with a little soda water/club soda and garnish with a lemon zest and a cherry. Serve at once.

PISCO SOUR

Not widely served, but delicious, this moreish cocktail relies on Pisco, a grape Brandy made and enjoyed in Peru and Chile. (Pictured on page 85 with Grapefruit Ceviche-style Shrimp Skewers, recipe page 135.)

50 ml/2 oz. pisco
25 ml/1 oz. lemon juice
15 ml/$\frac{1}{2}$ oz. sugar syrup
15 ml/$\frac{1}{2}$ oz. egg white
2 dashes of Angostura bitters

SERVES 1

Add all the ingredients to a cocktail shaker filled with ice cubes. Shake sharply and strain into a wine glass. Serve at once.

MOSCOW MULE

This is a refreshing cocktail, traditionally served in a copper mug that frosts with the icy chill of its contents. (Pictured with Crunchy Crab Salsa in Cucumber Boats, recipe page 118.)

15 ml/½ oz. lime juice
60 ml/2 oz. vodka, well chilled
10 ml/2 teaspoons sugar syrup
about 90 ml/3 oz. spicy ginger
　beer, well chilled
fresh mint sprig and lime wheels,
　to garnish

SERVES 1

Squeeze the lime juice into an ice-filled cocktail shaker.
　Add the vodka and sugar syrup and stir. Pour into a copper mug, add ice cubes, top up with ginger beer and garnish with a sprig of mint and a lime wheel. Serve at once. (Use mini copper mugs, as pictured, for 6 small, party-size servings.)

MINI MARGARITAS

Delight your guests with a down-sized version of a Mexican classic – the Margarita. No need to salt the rim of glasses for a crowd here if you serve the drinks with little skewers of lip-smacking Spicy Salt Lime Chicken (recipe page 121).

50 ml/1¹/₂ oz. silver tequila
30 ml/²/₃ oz. dry orange Curaçao
30 ml/²/₃ oz. lime juice
salt, for rimming the glass
　(optional, see recipe intro)

SERVES 2

Pour the tequila, Curaçao and lime juice into a cocktail shaker. Add a handful of ice cubes and shake vigorously for 10–15 seconds. Strain into a glasses (salt-rimmed, if liked) and serve at once.

NEGRONI ROYALE

A glamorous way to see in the New Year for those who find mere Champagne a little 'flat'. The Navy Gin brings some botanical power to help stand up against the other flavoursome ingredients, whilst the Campari and the vermouth add a balancing sweetness. Grapefruit bitters bring a lively zing to the mix, whilst the edible gold is one final, indulgent hint of decadence.

15 ml/^{1}/$_2$ oz. Hayman's Royal Dock Navy Gin
15 ml/^{1}/$_2$ oz. Campari
15 ml/^{1}/$_2$ oz. Martini Rosato
3 drops of grapefruit bitters
chilled sparkling white wine, to top up
edible gold flakes, to garnish

SERVES 1

Add the gin, Campari, vermouth, bitters and edible gold to a Champagne flute.

Top up with chilled sparkling wine. This allows the flakes of gold to dance up and down amongst the drink's bubbles. Serve at once.

ROSE & POMEGRANATE COSMO

A feast for the eyes as well as the tastebuds, this twist on the popular Cosmopolitan cocktail offers a little taste of the Levant with the addition of rose water and rose petals to garnish. (Pictured with Pitta Chips, Eggplant Caviar, Mint & Pomegranate, recipe page 144.)

35 ml/1¼ oz. vodka
20 ml/⅔ oz. triple sec
20 ml/⅔ oz. lemon juice
25 ml/1 oz. pomegranate juice
5 ml/1 teaspoon agave nectar
½ teaspoon rose water
fresh rose petals, to garnish

SERVES 1

Add all the ingredients to a cocktail shaker filled with ice cubes. Shake until chilled and then strain into a chilled martini glass. Garnish with rose petals and serve at once.

SWEDISH GLÖGG

Glögg translates as 'ember' and this is a drink for lovers of anything mulled. It is not practical to make in small quantities so this recipe makes 20 x 75-ml/3-oz. servings, perfect for creating a little 'hygge'. (Pictured with Cloudberry Jam Grilled Cheese, recipe page 133.)

peel of 1 small unwaxed orange
1 x 750-ml bottle red wine
375 ml/13 oz. ruby port
250 ml/1 cup brandy
2 tablespoons demerara/turbinado
   sugar
1 tablespoon whole cardamom
   pods, crushed
6 cloves
1 cinnamon stick
small raisins and slivered/sliced
   almonds, to garnish (optional)
20 small heatproof glasses

SERVES 20

Using metal tongs hold the orange peel over a flame on the hob/cooktop until it spots brown. Drop it into a large, heavy-based saucepan.

Add the wine, port, brandy, sugar and spices. Simmer over medium heat for about 20 minutes then strain into a heatproof jug/pitcher.

Pour into small heatproof glasses and add a few raisins and almond slivers to each serving to garnish. Serve with small coffee spoons, if liked.

APPLE PIE MOONSHINE

This is a particularly fun cocktail to serve at halloween and works well served in little glasses with handles. (Pictured page 24.)

100 ml/4 oz. apple pie moonshine
   (such as Midnight Moon)
100 ml/4 oz. cloudy apple juice/
   soft cider
50 ml/2 oz. cinnamon syrup
30 ml/1 oz. lemon juice
small green apple wedges, to garnish
cinnamon sticks, to garnish (optional)

SERVES 2

Pour all of the ingredients into an ice-filled cocktail shaker and shake until frosted. Pour into glasses and garnish with an apple wedge and a cinnamon stick. Serve at once.

FIRESIDE SANGRIA

Who said rosé wine was just for summer? Here is a delicious sparkling punch for colder days. It makes a refreshing and welcome alternative to the ubiquitous mulled wine at any festive gathering.

about 10 seedless white grapes, halved lengthways

about 10 seedless red grapes, halved lengthways

1 small orange, finely sliced

90 ml/3 oz. Grand Marnier, or other orange-flavoured liqueur

90 ml/3 oz. aged sweet red vermouth, such as Carpano Antica Formula

170 ml/^{3}/$_4$ cup clementine juice or blood orange juice

375 ml/1^1/$_2$ cups fresh, fruity Sauvignon Blanc

1 x 750-ml/25-oz. bottle well-chilled sparkling rosé, such as a pink Champagne or rosé Prosecco

dried orange slices and cinnamon sticks, to garnish

SERVES 6–8

Put the grapes and orange slices in a punch bowl. Pour in all of the other ingredients, including plenty of ice cubes and stir.

Serve ladled into ice-filled tumblers or red wine glasses and garnish each one with a dried orange slice and a cinnamon stick.

Winter gin & tonic

Gin and tonic is not normally associated with the colder winter months, but that doesn't mean that there aren't great drinks to enjoy, especially when well made. This uses a gin which has warm, spiced notes and in addition to tonic, there is ginger ale in the mix, too.

50 ml/1¾ oz. Warner Edwards Gin, or similar

75 ml/2½ oz. tonic water, ideally Schweppes

75 ml/2½ oz. ginger ale, ideally Schweppes

5 ml/1 teaspoon ginger wine or The King's Ginger Liqueur (optional)

an orange wedge studded with 3–4 cloves, extra cloves and a cinnamon stick, to garnish

SERVES 1

Start off with a clean glass, either a copa or balloon, as shown here, or a highball. Add fresh ice cubes to fill up the glass.

Stir gently for 15 seconds with a bar spoon or chopstick to chill the glass. Pour away any liquid from the melted ice. Top up the glass with more ice.

Add the gin, trying to ensure that you coat the ice as you pour. Add the tonic water. Pouring slowly helps the tonic to keep its fizz.

Add your garnish. Let rest for 30 seconds to allow the flavours to integrate with each other, then serve.

Note: Other good choices of gin include Portobello Road Gin and Edinburgh Gin.

CHRISTMAS GIN & TONIC

An alternative to Bucks Fizz or Champagne, this drink uses a gin which is made by distilling gin that has been infused with Christmas puddings. The tonic really brings out the rich spices and deep, fruity notes of the gin. For those in Australia, Four Pillars have also recently released a Christmas Pudding Gin.

150 ml/1¾ oz. Sacred Christmas Pudding Gin, or similar
150 ml/5 oz. tonic water, ideally Schweppes
a selection of dried fruit (cranberries, apricot, raisins), to garnish

SERVES 1

Start off with a clean glass, either a copa or balloon, as shown here, or a highball. Add fresh ice cubes to fill up the glass.

Stir gently for 15 seconds with a bar spoon or chopstick to chill the glass. Pour away any liquid from the melted ice. Top up the glass with more ice.

Add the gin, trying to ensure that you coat the ice as you pour. Add the tonic water. Pouring slowly helps the tonic to keep its fizz.

Add your garnish. Let rest for 30 seconds to allow the flavours to integrate with each other, then serve.

ALTERNATIVE RECIPE (ideal for Christmas Day morning)
20 ml/²⁄₃ oz. Sacred Christmas Pudding Gin/75 ml/ 2¹⁄₂ oz. Indian Tonic Water/orange peel, to garnish

Serve in a Champagne flute with a thin piece of orange peel to garnish.

New Year's Eve gin & tonic

The end of the year deserves a special celebratory gin tonic. This bright and crisp drink is a great way to say goodbye to one year and welcome in the next.

The drink uses Hammer & Son Old English Gin, which is lightly sweetened and has a full, spicy character. Even the bottle has a festive air, as the gin is packaged in old Champagne bottles. Fever-Tree Tonic Water has a pleasant crispness and the Brut Champagne adds both extra fizz and a little dryness.

50 ml/1³⁄₄ oz. Hammer & Son
   Old English Gin, or similar
200 ml/6³⁄₄ oz. tonic water,
   ideally Fever-Tree
50 ml/1³⁄₄ oz. Brut Champagne,
   or other dry sparkling wine
3 dashes of orange bitters
a flamed orange peel, to garnish

SERVES 1

Start off with a clean glass, either a copa or balloon, as shown here, or a highball. Add fresh ice cubes to fill up the glass.

Stir gently for 15 seconds with a bar spoon or chopstick to chill the glass. Pour away any liquid from the melted ice. Top up the glass with more ice.

Add the gin, trying to ensure that you coat the ice as you pour. Add the tonic water. Pouring slowly helps the tonic to keep its fizz.

Add your garnish. Let rest for 30 seconds to allow the flavours to integrate with each other, then serve.

DESSERT
COCKTAILS &
NIGHTCAPS

CHOCATINI

'A deliciously rich dessert cocktail, the perfect tipple for chocolate lovers and designed to be sipped slowly.

90 ml/3 oz. Bailey's Irish Cream
    Liqueur
30 ml/1 oz. dark crème de cacao
15 ml/½ oz. vodka
dark/bittersweet chocolate
    shavings, to garnish

SERVES 1

Pour all the ingredients into a cocktail shaker, add a handful of ice cubes and shake until frosted. Strain into a chilled Martini glass, sprinkle with dark chocolate shavings and serve at once.

HIBISCUS FIZZ

Hibiscus flowers are said to have health benefits, but never mind all that, let's put some in fizz! The flowers preserved in syrup are widely available now, and add a lovely reddish colour and sweet, fruity tang to your bubbles. Couldn't be easier or prettier.

1 hibiscus flower in syrup
a dash of Chambord or crème de framboise (optional)
well-chilled Prosecco, to top up

SERVES 1

Carefully place the hibiscus flower with the petals facing upwards in the bottom of a chilled Champagne flute. Add the Chambord, if using. Slowly pour in the Prosecco and serve at once.

ESPRESSO MARTINI

Use good freshly brewed coffee and you'll be rewarded with a foamy head on this modern classic.

25 ml/^{3}/$_4$ oz. freshly brewed
  strong espresso coffee
50 ml/1^2/$_3$ oz. vodka
25 ml/^{3}/$_4$ oz. Kahlúa or Tia Maria
  (coffee liqueurs)
7.5 ml/^{1}/$_2$ tablespoon sugar syrup
3 coffee beans, to garnish
  (optional)

SERVES 1

Pour all the ingredients into a cocktail shaker filled with ice cubes and shake vigorously. Strain into a Martini glass. Wait for the cocktail to 'separate' – a foam will rise to the top and the liquid below will become clearer. Garnish with coffee beans (if liked) and serve at once.

ALMOND ESPRESSO MARTINI

This variation is composed of Amaretto liqueur and vodka as well as a coffee liqueur, delicious served with marzipan.

25 ml/^{3}/$_4$ oz. freshly brewed
  strong espresso coffee
35 ml/1^1/$_4$ oz. vodka
20 ml/^{2}/$_3$ oz. Amaretto Disaronno
  (almond liqueur)
15 ml/^{1}/$_2$ oz. Kahlúa or Tia Maria
  (coffee liqueurs)
3 coffee beans and a pinch of
  toasted, flaked/slivered
  almonds, to garnish (optional)

SERVES 1

Pour all the ingredients into a cocktail shaker filled with ice cubes and shake vigorously. Strain into a Martini glass. Wait for the cocktail to 'separate' – a foam will rise to the top and the liquid below will become clearer. Garnish with the coffee beans and almonds (if liked) and serve at once.

Black Russian

Black and White Russians are classic cocktails that have been on the scene for many years. They make stylish after-dinner drinks with their sweet coffee flavour, which is sharpened by the vodka.

50 ml/1²/₃ oz. vodka
25 ml/³/₄ oz. Kahlúa
(coffee liqueur)
a stemmed cherry, to garnish

SERVES 1

Combine the vodka and Kahlúa in a mixing glass with a handful of ice cubes. Stir to chill and strain into a rocks glass filled with fresh ice cubes. Garnish with a stemmed cherry and serve at once.

White Russian

The White Russian, with its addition of the cream float, is great served as an indulgent and festive nightcap.

50 ml/1²/₃ oz. vodka
25 ml/³/₄ oz. Kahlúa
(coffee liqueur)
25 ml/³/₄ oz. single/light cream,
chilled
a stemmed cherry, to garnish

SERVES 1

Simply make a Black Russian (see above) then layer the chilled cream into the glass over the back of a long-handled barspoon. Garnish with a stemmed cherry and serve at once.

Prosecco Cosmopolitan

THE classic girls' night out cocktail given extra festive pep with Prosecco! (Pictured page 96, front.)

25 ml/1 oz. vodka
50 ml/2 oz. cranberry juice
5 ml/1 teaspoon lime juice
well-chilled Prosecco, to top up
a strip of orange zest, to garnish

SERVES 1

Put the vodka, cranberry juice and lime juice in a cocktail shaker with a handful of ice cubes. Shake well and strain into a chilled martini glass. Top up with Prosecco. Squeeze the orange zest strip in half lengthways so that the essential oils in the skin spritz on to the drink, then drop it in. Serve at once.

Prima Donna

A dazzling pomegranate and limoncello number. Quite a performance and a fun way to end any evening. (Pictured page 96, back.)

25 ml/1 oz. vodka
15 ml/½ oz. limoncello
25 ml/1 oz. pomegranate juice
1 teaspoon lemon bursting bubbles
    (optional), see page 4
well-chilled Prosecco, to top up

SERVES 1

Put the vodka, limoncello and pomegranate juice in a cocktail shaker and add a handful of ice cubes. Shake well and strain into a chilled Champagne flute. Add the bursting bubbles, if using, then top with Prosecco and serve at once.

CHERRY BABY

Bakewell tart in a glass – lovers of cherry and almond will be delighted with this sweet treat. (Pictured page 97, back.)

25 ml/1 oz. Amaretto
15 ml/¹/₂ oz. cherry brandy
25 ml/1 oz. cherry juice, or the syrup from a can of cherries
well-chilled Prosecco, to top up
cocktail cherries, to garnish

SERVES 1

Put the Amaretto, cherry brandy and cherry juice in a cocktail shaker and add a handful of ice cubes. Shake well, then strain into an old-fashioned glass. Top up with Prosecco and serve at once.

STILETTO

Simple but delicious, and a new way to enjoy the classic after-dinner favourite, Amaretto diSaronno. (Pictured page 97, front.)

25 ml/1 oz. Amaretto
15 ml/¹/₂ oz. lime juice
well-chilled Prosecco, to top up
a lime slice, to garnish

MAKES 1

Put the clementine segments into a cocktail shaker with the Cointreau. Muddle well, then add the pomegranate juice and a handful of ice cubes and shake well. Strain into a chilled Champagne flute and add the pomegranate seeds, if using. Pour in the Prosecco and serve at once.

BLACK MANHATTAN

This twist on the Manhattan foregoes the traditional vermouth, putting Amaro Averna front and centre. The recipe is adapted from a cocktail created by Todd Smith at Bourbon & Branch in San Francisco.

60 ml/2 oz. Bulleit Rye Whiskey
15 ml/^{1}/$_2$ oz. Amaro Averna
15 ml/^{1}/$_2$ oz. amontillado sherry
5 ml/1 teaspoon Pedro Ximénez
    sherry
2 dashes of chocolate bitters
an orange zest and a pitted fresh
    cherry, to garnish

SERVES 1

Combine all the drink ingredients in a mixing glass with a scoop of cubed ice. Stir for about 20 seconds before straining into a chilled coupe glass. Squeeze the orange zest to express the citrus oils over the drink. Garnish the glass with the orange zest and a fresh cherry dropped into the drink. Serve at once.

BROOKLYN

A variation of the Manhattan named after the neighbouring borough. Replace the Amer Picon here with Cynar, and you've got a Bensonhurst, an equally delectable and sophisticated cocktail.

45 ml/1^1/$_2$ oz. Rittenhouse
    100 Proof Rye Whiskey
15 ml/^{1}/$_2$ oz. Noilly Prat Dry,
    or other dry vermouth
5 ml/1 teaspoon Amer Picon
5 ml/1 teaspoon Luxardo
    Maraschino Cherry Liqueur
a lemon zest, to serve
a Luxardo maraschino cherry,
    to garnish

SERVES 1

Combine all the drink ingredients in a mixing glass with a scoop of cubed ice. Stir for about 30 seconds before straining into a chilled coupette glass. Squeeze the lemon zest to express the citrus oils over the drink and discard. Garnish with a cherry and serve at once.

Snowgroni

Advocaat is a liqueur made from sugar and eggs (much like eggnog) with a creamy, custard-like consistency. The festive Snowball cocktail is traditionally mixed with Advocaat and lemonade, with the latter adding a refreshing quality that balances out the liqueur's richness.

    Here this hybrid of two classic cocktails – the retro Snowball and the perennial Negroni – balances the rich creaminess of Advocaat with the bittersweet intensity of a Negroni.

15 ml/½ oz. Conker Dorset Dry Gin,
   or other dry gin
15 ml/½ oz. red vermouth
15 ml/½ oz. Campari
30 ml/1 oz. Advocaat
150 ml/5 oz. sparkling clear
   lemonade
a lime wedge and cocktail cherry,
   to garnish

SERVES 1

Add the gin, vermouth, Campari and Advocaat to an ice-filled highball glass and stir. Top up with chilled lemonade and garnish with a lime wedge and a cocktail cherry to serve at once.

IRISH COFFEE

An after dinner cocktail that needs little introduction, the Irish coffee is thought to have been first created at Foynes Airbase, near Limerick, Ireland, in the early 1940s. The drink was later popularized in the US at the Buena Vista Café in San Francisco. (Pictured opposite.)

45 ml/1½ oz. Jameson Caskmates Stout Edition Whiskey, or other Irish whiskey
20 ml/⅔ oz. Demerara/turbinado sugar syrup, or to taste
100 ml/3⅓ oz. hot coffee
30 ml/1 oz. double/heavy cream
freshly grated nutmeg, to garnish (optional)

SERVES 1

Mix together the whisky, sugar syrup and coffee in an Irish Coffee glass. Place the double/heavy cream in a bowl and whisk until slightly thickened. Using a warm spoon, pour the cream over the top of the drink, creating a foamy 'head.' Garnish with freshly grated nutmeg, if you like, and serve at once.

CINNAMON BUTTERED RUM

Buttered rum just sounds so good doesn't it? The traditional recipe is diluted with water but here it's served neat in a small glass and made with an oak-aged dark rum, flavoured with warming spices, including cinnamon. (Pictured page 151.)

25 g/1½ tablespoons butter
2 tablespoons demerera/turbinado sugar
4 cinnamon sticks
200 ml/¾ cup spiced gold rum, such as Captain Morgan's Spiced
2 small glass tankards

SERVES 4

Gently heat the butter, demerera sugar and cinnamon sticks in a saucepan until the butter has melted and the sugar dissolved. Stir in the rum, transfer to a heatproof jug/pitcher and then pour into heatproof serving glasses. Garnish each serving with a cinnamon stick and serve at once.

Irish flip

The flip is one of the oldest categories of mixed drinks – here we have an Irish take on the classic. Flips were originally served hot, but this drink actually works equally well cold. Similar to eggnog, it's a good drink to serve during the festive season. (Pictured opposite.)

50 ml/1²/₃ oz. Jameson Irish Whiskey, or other Irish whiskey
25 ml/³/₄ oz. Guinness Stout Reduction Syrup*
1 whole egg
10 ml/2 teaspoons Pedro Ximénez sherry
freshly grated nutmeg, to garnish

SERVES 1

Add all the drink ingredients to a cocktail shaker with a scoop of ice and shake hard. Single-strain into a wine glass with no ice. Garnish with grated nutmeg.

*To make Guinness Stout Reduction Syrup:
500 ml/2 cups Guinness, 250 ml/1 cup Demerara/ turbinado sugar

Put the Guinness in a saucepan and simmer over a medium heat for 30–40 minutes until the volume is reduced by half. Add the sugar and stir until dissolved. Remove from the heat and allow to cool before bottling and refrigerating. Use within 1 month.

Brandy Alexander

Here is a classic rich and creamy cocktail that particularly benefits from being served in a small portion, perhaps in place of a dessert. Alternatively, serve this as an elegant, and somewhat easier to prepare, alternative to eggnog. (Pictured on page 63.)

60 ml/2 oz. cognac
30 ml/1 oz. dark crème de cacao
30 ml/1 oz. single/light cream
freshly grated nutmeg, to garnish

SERVES 2

Pour all of the ingredients into an ice-filled cocktail shaker and shake until frosted. Pour into cocktail glasses and garnish with a dusting of freshly grated nutmeg and serve at once.

Canapés & small bites

Cheese Straws

These cheese straws are the perfect accompaniment to a glass of chilled Champagne at a festive gathering. You can vary the recipe in a variety of ways, topping with seeds or spices, or adding chopped herbs or tangy blue cheese to the pastry.

160 g/1⅓ cups plain/all-purpose flour, sifted, plus extra for dusting

100 g/¾ cup fine golden/yellow polenta/cornmeal

salt and freshly ground black pepper

2 eggs

100 g/6½ tablespoons butter, softened

250 g/1¾ cups finely grated cheddar cheese

1 teaspoon smoked paprika, plus extra for sprinkling

1 tablespoon cream cheese

poppy seeds, for sprinkling (optional)

2 baking sheets, greased and lined with baking parchment

MAKES 20

Preheat the oven to 180°C (350°F) Gas 4.

Place the flour and polenta in a bowl and mix together. Season with salt and pepper. Beat one of the eggs and add to the flour mixture, along with the butter, three quarters of the cheddar cheese, the smoked paprika and the cream cheese. Mix together to form a soft dough using a stand mixer or whisk.

On a flour-dusted surface, roll out half of the dough using a rolling pin to a rectangle about 20 x 12 cm/8 x 5 inches in size. Cut it into 10 straws approximately 2 cm/¾ inch wide and 12 cm/5 inches long. Carefully transfer the straws to the baking sheets, using a spatula. Repeat with the remaining dough, adding a little water if it has dried out, to prevent it from cracking.

Beat the second egg, and brush over the tops of the straws using a pastry brush. Sprinkle over the chopped pecans and the reserved cheddar cheese. Add some poppy seeds, or use poppy seeds in place of the pecans, if you prefer. Season with salt, pepper and a little extra smoked paprika.

Bake in the preheated oven for 10–15 minutes, until golden brown. Remove from the oven and leave to cool on the baking sheets before serving. The straws are best eaten on the day they are made, although they will keep for up to 2 days in an airtight container.

Parmesan & sweet paprika biscuits

These delicate mouthfuls bring the classic cheese biscuit right up to date. They are smoky, dry and moreish and go perfectly with a glass of Prosecco. Be careful not to overcook them, or they may taste bitter. (Pictured opposite.)

125 g/scant 2 cups Parmesan cheese, finely grated
125 g/¹/₂ cup plus 1 tablespoon chilled butter, cut into small cubes
125 g/1 cup minus 1 tablespoon plain/all-purpose flour, plus extra for dusting
2 teaspoons sweet paprika
2 teaspoons Dijon mustard
¹/₂ teaspoon sea salt
freshly ground black pepper

4.5-cm/1³/₄-in. plain cookie cutter
2 baking sheets
baking parchment

MAKES 40 BISCUITS

Put all the ingredients in a food processor and process briefly until the mixture forms a dough ball. Wrap the dough in baking parchment and chill in the fridge for 1 hour.

Preheat the oven to 200°C (400°F) Gas 6.

Dust the work surface and a rolling pin with flour and roll out the dough to approximately 5 mm/¹/₃ in. thick. Using a 4.5-cm/1³/₄-in. plain cookie cutter, stamp out 40 biscuits and put them on baking sheets. Bake in the preheated oven for 8 minutes, checking after 6 minutes to make sure the biscuits are not darkening in colour.

Remove from the oven, leave for a couple of minutes, then very carefully lift the biscuits onto a wire rack to cool and crisp up before serving.

Anchovy wafers

Ready-made salty snacks pall beside these crumbly melt-in-the-mouth wafers. They deserve to be paired with well-chilled dry Champagne.

125 g/1 cup minus 1 tablespoon plain/all-purpose flour
125 g/¹/₂ cup plus 1 tablespoon chilled butter, cut into small cubes
125 g/1¹/₂ cups strong mature/sharp cheddar cheese, grated
2 tablespoons chopped fresh sweet marjoram or 2 teaspoons dried oregano
100-g/3¹/₂-oz.can anchovies in olive oil, drained and halved lengthways
freshly ground black pepper

2 baking sheets
baking parchment

MAKES ABOUT 40

Sift the flour onto a clean work surface, make a well in the centre and add the butter, cheese, herbs and black pepper. With clean, cool fingers, rub together to form a soft, tacky dough. Scoop the dough up, with the aid of a spatula if necessary, and put it on a large piece of baking parchment. Mould the mixture into a flattish rectangle, wrap up in the greaseproof paper and chill for 1 hour in the fridge.

Preheat the oven to 200°C (400°C) Gas 6. Using a sharp knife, cut the dough (just as you would slice a loaf of bread) into thin wafers and arrange them on baking sheets, positioning them noit too close together. Lay an anchovy half lengthways on each wafer and bake for 8 minutes until golden. Let cool on a wire rack.

HOME-MADE MINI OATCAKES WITH HONEY
ROAST SALMON FLAKES & GINGER BUTTER

These crumbly homemade oatcakes, spread with a warming fresh ginger butter, and topped with roast salmon flakes make a deliciously indulgent and substantial canapé for winter parties. (Pictured opposite with a Rusty Nail, recipe page 25.)

100 g/3½ oz. butter, softened
20 g/¾ oz. fresh ginger, finely grated
140 g/5 oz. hot smoked honey roast salmon flakes
snipped chives, to garnish
freshly ground black pepper

OATCAKES
125 g/4½ oz. wholemeal/whole-wheat flour
150 g/5½ oz. oatmeal, plus extra for dusting
150 g/5½ oz. rolled/old-fashioned oats
1½ teaspoons baking powder
1 teaspoon salt
1 tablespoon soft brown sugar
125 g/4½ oz. butter, melted
4-cm/1½-inch round cookie cutter
baking sheet lined with baking parchment

MAKES 20

To make the oatcakes, preheat the oven to 160°C (325°F) Gas 3.

Combine all the dry ingredients in a bowl. Pour in the melted butter and mix. Add 3 tablespoons water, a little at a time, kneading into a firm dough.

Halve the dough and roll out each piece on an oatmeal-dusted surface to a 3-mm/⅛-inch thickness. Use the cutter to stamp out 20 rounds and place on the prepared baking sheet.

Bake in the preheated oven for 15 minutes. Let cool on a wire rack.

For the honey roast salmon topping, beat the softened butter with the ginger. Spread a little butter on each cooled oatcake and top with a few pieces of flaked salmon. Top with a sprinkle of chives and a grinding of black pepper and serve.

Beetroot Rosti with Horseradish Cream & Dill

A warm beetroot/beet rosti is served topped with a horseradish cream and aniseedy dill garnish. A whole smorgasbord of Scandi fun and flavour in just a few mouthfuls. (Pictured opposite with a Snap Apple, recipe page 60.)

250 g/9 oz. cooked beetroot/beet, grated

250 g/9 oz. raw potato, grated and
    squeezed dry

1 tablespoon plain/all-purpose flour

1 egg, beaten

salt and pepper

2 tablespoons sunflower oil

150 ml/5½ oz. sour cream or crème fraiche

1 tablespoon hot horseradish sauce

sea salt and freshly ground black pepper

fresh dill, to garnish

4.5-cm/1¾-inch cookie cutter

MAKES 20

Mix the grated beetroot/beet, potato, flour and egg together and season well with salt and pepper.

Heat 1 tablespoon of the oil in a medium non-stick frying pan/skillet. Spread half the mixture across the base of the frying pan/skillet (about 5 mm/¼ inch thick). Reduce the heat to low and cook for about 10 minutes on both sides, until both sides are crisp and golden. (Use a plate to tip and flip over.)

Remove from the pan and cool slightly on kitchen towels. Heat the remaining oil and repeat with the rest of the mixture. Use the cookie cutter to stamp 10 rounds from each rosti cake. Let cool completely.

Mix the cream and horseradish together in a small bowl and season to taste. Spoon a little on top of each rosti and garnish with dill. Serve at room temperature rather than cold.

Parsnip & Apple Remoulade
WITH BAYONNE HAM ON RYE

2 raw parsnips, peeled and grated

1 Granny Smith, grated

finely grated zest and freshly squeezed
    juice of 1 lemon

100 ml/scant ⅓ cup crème fraîche
    or sour cream

2 tablespoons good-quality mayonnaise

1 teaspoon wholegrain or Dijon mustard

sea salt and freshly ground black pepper

4 slices of rye bread/pumpernickel,
    cut into 4-cm/1½-inch squares

70 g/3 oz. air-dried cured ham,
    such as Bayonne (optional)

a handful of flat-leaf parsley leaves,
    finely chopped

MAKES ABOUT 24

Parsnips and apples flavour pair beautifully in this simple French-style remoulade used to top small squares of rye bread. The Bayonne ham is optional here. (Pictured page 49).

Combine the grated parsnips and apple in a large bowl and add the lemon juice and toss.

In a separate bowl mix together the lemon zest, crème fraîche, mayonnaise and mustard and stir to combine. Season to taste with salt and pepper.

Spoon a little remoulade onto each bread square, top with a small piece of ham (if using) and garnish with a sprinkle of flat-leaf parsley to serve.

Smoked salmon mousse croustades

A rich smoked salmon mousse is spooned into a crisp croustade made from bread for an elegant canapé. (Pictured opposite with a Chelsea Sidecar, recipe page 49).

SMOKED SALMON MOUSSE
100 g/3^1/$_2$ oz. smoked salmon
freshly squeezed juice of 1 lemon
freshly ground black pepper
150 ml/^{2}/$_3$ cup double/heavy cream
4 slices mild smoked salmon, cut into strips
finely chopped dill, to garnish

CROUSTADES
5 large slices of medium-thickness sliced
    white bread, crusts cut off
2 tablespoons light olive oil
5-cm/2-inch round cookie cutter
24-hole mini muffin pan

MAKES 20

First make the croustades. Preheat the oven to 180°C (350°F) Gas 4. Using a rolling pin, press down heavily onto each slice of bread in turn to roll it out thinly. Brush each flattened slice with oil. Use the cutter to stamp out about 4 rounds per slice. Push each round in the holes of the muffin pan. Bake in the preheated oven for 10 minutes, until lightly coloured and crisp. Allow to cool on a wire rack before filling.

To make the smoked salmon mousse, put the salmon in a food processor with the lemon juice and season with freshly ground black pepper and blitz until the salmon is finely chopped. Add the cream and blitz again until you have a smooth mousse. Store in the fridge until you are ready to serve. To assemble, spoon the mousse into each croustade, top with a piece of smoked salmon. Sprinkle with dill and serve.

Crunchy crab salsa in cucumber boats

Simple to make and refreshing, enjoy these cooling cucumber and crab 'boats' in an overheated party room. They are also a useful gluten-free option for your guests. (Pictured on page 69.)

2 long, thin cucumbers
250 g/1 cup white crab meat, ideally fresh
100 g/scant ^{1}/$_2$ cup fromage frais
100 g/3^1/$_2$ oz. radishes, finely chopped
2 tablespoons small capers, rinsed
1 tablespoon scissored chives
2 tablespoons light olive oil
2 tablespoons ginger wine
salt and freshly ground black pepper
20 cocktail picks or forks, to serve

MAKES ABOUT 20

For the cucumber boats, peel each cucumber. Cut off the rounded ends and cut it in half lengthways. Use a teaspoon to scrape out the seeds. Slice a thin strip off the bottom of each half to create a flat base. Slice the remaining flesh crossways at 3–4 cm/1^1/$_4$–1^1/$_2$-inch intervals to create about 20 generous crescents.

Mix the crab meat and fromage frais in a small bowl. Cover and chill. Put the radishes, capers, chives, olive oil and ginger wine in a separate bowl and mix. Season to taste with salt and pepper. To assemble, spoon a little crab mixture into each cucumber boat and top with some of the salsa. Thread a cocktails pick through from side to side or serve with cocktail forks.

SPICY MEXICAN CORN
& QUESO FRESCA QUESADILLA WEDGES

Perfect party food, these crisply toasted quesadillas ooze spicy melted cheese and corn.
(Pictured opposite with a Paloma, recipe page 63.)

4 small flour tortillas/sandwich wraps
   (each 18 cm/7 inches diameter)
75 g/3 oz. Mexican queso fresca or mild feta,
   crumbled
100 g/4 oz. Gruyère, grated
4 tablespoons canned sweetcorn,
   drained and rinsed
30 g/1 oz. coriander/cilantro leaves,
   finely chopped
4–6 spring onions/scallions
1 large green chilli/chile, deseeded
   and finely chopped
salt and freshly ground pepper
4 tablespoons olive oil, for shallow frying

MAKES 20

Place 2 of the tortillas on a work surface. Divide the cheeses, sweetcorn, coriander/cilantro, spring onions/scallions and chopped chilli/chile and season well with salt and pepper. Press the remaining tortillas on top to make a sandwich. Heat 2 tablespoons olive oil in a large frying pan/skillet over medium heat. Fry the quesadillas one at a time on both sides until light golden and crisp (use a metal fish slice to press them down while cooking and to turn them over). Cut each one into 12 small wedges and serve warm.

SPICY SALT LIME CHICKEN

Something good happens when you put chilli, lime and salt together.
Whet appetites with these zingy bites. (Pictured page 71.)

500 g/18 oz. skinless, boneless
   chicken thighs
3 tablespoons light olive oil
2 generous pinches of chilli/chile
   sea salt flakes
finely grated zest and freshly squeezed
   juice of 2 unwaxed limes
lime wedges, to garnish
non-reactive shallow dish
cocktail picks, to serve

MAKES 40

Cut the chicken into 40 even-size chunks and put it in the non-reactive dish with 1 tablespoon of the olive oil, a pinch of the chilli/chile sea salt flakes and the zest and juice of 1 lime.

Let marinate in the fridge for 2 hours. When you are ready to cook, remove the chicken from the marinade. Heat the remaining olive oil in a frying pan/skillet and sauté the chicken over medium heat for about 5 minutes until cooked through, shaking the pan occasionally.

Put in a clean dish with the remaining salt and lime zest and juice. Mix and chill for 1 hour before serving on cocktail picks.

Maple-Roasted Squash & Whipped Ricotta Bruschetta with Sage

Bruschetta toasts are easy to make and make a base for robust toppings.
Here squash is roasted with maple sugar and topped with whipped ricotta
(Pictured opposite with Apple Pie Moonshine, recipe page 76.)

3½ tablespoons olive oil,
   plus extra for brushing
   the bruschetta
1½ teaspoons maple sugar
   (or soft brown sugar)
450-g/1-lb. butternut squash,
   peeled, seeded and cut in
   1.5 cm/½ inch cubes
1 slim baguette/French stick
24 fresh sage leaves
about 165 g/¾ cup fresh ricotta
½ teaspoon freshly grated lemon
   zest and freshly squeezed
   lemon juice, to taste
sea salt and freshly ground
   black pepper

baking sheets

MAKES ABOUT 24

Preheat the oven to 180°C (350°F) Gas 4. Put 2 tablespoons
of the oil in a bowl with the maple sugar and add the squash
cubes. Toss to coat.

Tip out onto a baking sheet in a single layer and roast in
the preheated oven for 20–25 minutes, until golden and tender.

Preheat the grill/broiler. Thinly slice the baguette on an
angle to create long, narrow fingers, drizzle with oil and grill/
broil until crispy on both sides. (These toasts can be made
a few hours ahead of serving.)

Heat the remaining oil in a small skillet over medium/high
heat. Add the sage leaves and cook until they curl and are
dark green. Use a slotted spoon to remove them from the
pan and put on paper towels to drain.

Beat the ricotta and lemon zest until light and airy
and season with lemon juice, salt and pepper. Spread each
bruschetta with ricotta, top with a few cubes of squash
and finish with a fried sage leaf.

SPANISH MEN

30 small Spanish olives, pitted
1 tablespoon extra virgin olive oil
1 tablespoon sherry vinegar
1 teaspoon smoked paprika
100 g/3½ oz. Serrano ham, thinly sliced
1 tablespoon very finely chopped fresh
    flat-leaf parsley
150 g/5½ oz. membrillo (quince paste),
    cut into 30 identically-sized cubes
150 g/5½ oz. manchego cheese, cut into
    30 identically-sized cubes
cocktail picks

MAKES 30

These perfect, savoury bites need no cooking and can be assembled well in advance and kept chilled until ready to serve.

Begin by marinating the olives in the olive oil, sherry vinegar and smoked paprika for an hour or so.

Lay out the Serrano ham and rub the parsley over each slice. Cut into 30 equal-sized pieces (approximately 3 pieces from each slice). Roll up each small piece as tightly as possible into a cylinder and chill for 20 minutes.

Assemble the men by threading the components onto a cocktail pick in the following order: an olive, a cube of membrillo, a roll of ham and a cube of manchego.

HOT CRUMBED SHRIMP WITH TOMATO AÏOLI

TOMATO AÏOLI
3 egg yolks
2 garlic cloves
70 g/2½ oz. sun-dried or sun-blush
    tomatoes in oil, drained
freshly squeezed juice of 1 lemon
1 teaspoon tomato purée/paste
500 ml/2 cups olive oil

HOT CRUMBED PRAWNS
100 g/1¾ cups fresh breadcrumbs
400 g/14 oz. king prawns/jumbo shrimp,
    uncooked, peeled
grated zest and freshly squeezed juice
    of 2 unwaxed lemons
lemon wedges, to serve
sea salt
cocktail picks

MAKES 40

Eat these lemon-drenched prawns/shrimp hot or cold with sweet tomato aïoli and bring a distinctly Spanish feel to any party, when served with the Spanish Men (see above).

Preheat the grill/broiler to high.

Put all the aïoli ingredients, except the olive oil, in a food processor and blend. With the motor running, gradually trickle in the oil, very slowly at first, until you have a silky thick mayonnaise. Pour into a serving bowl.

For the prawns/shrimp, lightly toast the breadcrumbs under the hot grill/broiler until crisp and golden. Watch carefully and do not let them burn. Combine the prawns/shrimp with the lemon zest and half the lemon juice in a bowl. Transfer the prawns/shrimp to a baking sheet and grill/broil for 2–3 minutes, turning once, until they have turned from blue to pink.

Quickly pile the prawns/shrimp onto a serving plate. Sprinkle the remaining lemon juice over, season with a little sea salt and scatter the toasted breadcrumbs over the top. Serve immediately with lemon wedges, cocktail sticks/toothpicks and the tomato aïoli for dipping.

CAESAR SALAD TARTLETS

13 slices fresh white bread
50 ml/3^1/$_2$ tablespoons olive oil, shaken with 1
    crushed garlic clove and 1 teaspoon sea salt
100 g/3^1/$_2$ oz. anchovy fillets, chopped
    quite finely
1 garlic clove, crushed
1 tablespoon freshly chopped dill
1 tablespoon freshly chopped mint
200 g/7 oz. Little Gem/Boston lettuce,
    finely shredded
grated zest and freshly squeezed juice
    of 1 unwaxed lime
1–2 egg yolks (optional)
100 g/1^1/$_3$ cups Parmesan cheese, finely grated
freshly ground black pepper
5^1/$_2$-cm/2^1/$_4$-in. plain cookie cutter
4 or 5 x 12-hole mini muffin pans

MAKES 40–50

The perfect canapé for those who like the croûton bit of caesar salad best. Here the croûton is the star, with the salad cradled within. Use Little Gem/Boston lettuces, as they hold their bite and freshness well, even when chopped. (Pictured opposite.)

Preheat the oven to 200°C (400°F) Gas 6.

Use the cookie cutter to cut 3 or 4 rounds out of each slice of bread. Brush each round with the garlic oil and press into mini muffin pans. Bake in the preheated oven for about 6 minutes until golden brown and toasted.

Put any remaining garlic oil in a large bowl with all the other ingredients, except the Parmesan, and toss together.

Finally, sprinkle the Parmesan into the salad to coat everything finely and pile into the croûton cases.

ENDIVE CUPS WITH ROQUEFORT MOUSSE, PEAR & CANDIED WALNUTS

1 tablespoon butter
60 g/^{1}/$_4$ cup white sugar
140 g/1 cup walnut halves
125 g/4^1/$_2$ oz. Roquefort cheese
125 g/4^1/$_2$ oz. cream cheese
salt and freshly ground black pepper
1 large ripe Anjou or Bartlett pear, peeled
    and finely diced
a little freshly squeezed lemon juice
20 small endive leaves, washed and
    patted dry

MAKES 20

There is no better way to enjoy tangy blue cheese than with bitter endive, sweet pear and walnuts. (Pictured page 22.)

First make the candied walnuts. Heat a non-stick pan/skillet over medium heat and add the butter, sugar and walnuts. Heat for about 5 minutes, stirring constantly until the sugar and butter have melted and the nuts are toasted and well coated in the mixture. Tip them onto a tray lined with parchment paper and quickly separate. Leave to cool. Beat the Roquefort and the cream cheese together until blended and whipped. Season to taste with salt and pepper. Peel and finely dice the pear. Squeeze a little lemon juice over the dice.

To assemble, spoon blue cheese mousse into each endive cup, add a few pieces of diced pear and top with a caramelized walnut.

Slow-roasted Tomato Galettes
with Black Olive Tapenade & Goats' Cheese

20–25 baby plum tomatoes
1 tablespoon caster/superfine sugar
400 g/14 oz. ready-rolled puff pastry,
    thawed if frozen
4 tablespoons olive oil
150 g/5^1/$_2$ oz. goats' cheese log with rind
    (not too ripe)
freshly ground black pepper
small fresh basil leaves, to serve

BLACK OLIVE TAPENADE
100 g/1 cup pitted black olives
20 g/2 tablespoons capers
1 tablespoon anchovy paste
1 garlic clove, crushed
1 tablespoon olive oil
1 teaspoon sea salt
1 teaspoon freshly chopped thyme
oiled baking sheets
4-cm/1^1/$_2$-in. plain cookie cutter

MAKES 40–50

These stacks of sweet tomatoes, savoury tapenade and tangy goats' cheese taste as good as they look. (Pictured opposite.)

Preheat the oven to 140°C (275°F) Gas 1.

Cut the baby plum tomatoes in half lengthways, season with the sugar and black pepper and put on an oiled baking sheet. Bake in the preheated oven for 2 hours. Remove the tomatoes from the oven and leave to cool.

Turn the oven temperature up to 200°C (400°F) Gas 6.

Brush the puff pastry with the olive oil, prick all over with a fork and stamp out 40–50 discs using a 4-cm/1^1/$_2$-in. plain cookie cutter and put them on baking sheets. Bake for 10–15 minutes, turning over halfway through. Remove from the oven but leave the heat on.

Put all the tapenade ingredients in a food processor and blend to mix. Cover and set aside until needed. Thinly slice the goats' cheese into 40–50 rounds or pieces depending on the diameter of the log (to make this easier, chill the cheese beforehand).

To assemble the galettes, spread a little tapenade onto each cooked pastry disc. Top with a goats' cheese slice and tomato half. Return to the oven for about 5 minutes to warm through, then serve topped with a basil leaf.

Goats' Cheese & Pink Peppercorn Balls

200-g/8-oz. soft goats' cheese log
3 tablespoons crushed pink peppercorns
16 seedless green grapes
16 cocktails picks, to serve

MAKES 16

A great no-cook recipe that simple involves rolling a soft goats' cheese into balls and then in fragrant pink peppercorns and add a fresh grape for a burst of fresh flavour. (Pictured page 41.)

Cut the goats' cheese log into 16 pieces and roll these into balls. Roll the balls in the crushed pink peppercorns. Insert a cocktail pick into a grape and add the ball. Keep refrigerated until ready to serve.

FLASH-SEARED TUNA ON RYE
WITH HORSERADISH & TARRAGON CREAM

2 tablespoons olive oil

1 teaspoon soft brown sugar

500 g/1 lb. 2 oz. piece of fresh tuna loin,
   thin end

200 ml/1 cup crème fraîche

2 tablespoons horseradish sauce

1 carrot, grated

2 tablespoons freshly chopped tarragon,
   plus 20 whole leaves to serve

300 g/10½ oz. rye bread, cut into 20 fingers

sea salt and freshly ground black pepper

a griddle pan

MAKES 20

Fresh tuna is complemented here by the sharpness of the horseradish and the aniseed pungency of tarragon. With the rye bread base, this is a substantial canapé. (Pictured opposite.)

In a wide, shallow bowl, mix the olive oil, sugar and a little salt and black pepper together, then add the tuna loin and turn carefully until coated.

Heat a heavy-based griddle pan over a high heat until very hot. Add the tuna and, using tongs to turn it over, sear on all sides for about 1 minute. Remove from the heat and let it cool slightly before cutting into 20 thin, even slices.

Mix the crème fraîche, horseradish, carrot and chopped tarragon together in a separate bowl. Season with salt and black pepper and spread on the rye bread fingers. Top each with a slice of seared tuna and a tarragon leaf and serve immediately.

VERMOUTH SCALLOPS WITH GREEN OLIVE TAPENADE

500 g/18 oz. fresh scallops (30–40)

3 tablespoons dry vermouth

2 tablespoons olive oil

90 g/¾ cup green olives, stoned/pitted

3 spring onions/scallions, chopped

1 garlic clove

1 tablespoon chopped fresh parsley

1 cured chorizo sausage
   (about 300 g/10½ oz.)

sea salt and freshly ground black pepper

a griddle pan

cocktail picks

MAKES 30–40

Confirmed Martini lovers will enjoy this one (see recipe page 10); it's a fitting canapé to kick off a party. These can be served on cocktail picks or on slices of cucumber; one large cucumber is sufficient for this quantity of scallops.

Put the scallops in a large bowl with 1 tablespoon of the vermouth, the olive oil and a pinch of salt and black pepper and let sit for 10 minutes.

Heat a griddle pan over a high heat until very hot and sear the scallops for 1 minute on each side. Do not move the scallops during cooking, or they will tear.

Put all the remaining ingredients accept the chorizo, in a food processor with ½ teaspoon salt and give it a few short sharp blasts until the tapenade mixture looks chopped but not too mushy. Slice the chorizo so you have a slice for each scallop (not too thinly as you want it to support the weight of the scallops).

To assemble, spoon a little tapenade onto each chorizo slice, put a seared scallop on top and secure with a cocktail pick to serve.

BRIE & CRANBERRY SAUCE PUFFS

Ready-made puff pastry dough makes a great freezer stand-by when you need an impressive party canapé in a hurry. Topped with Brie and cranberry sauce they make a deliciously festive and indulgent mouthful. (Pictured page 60.)

375-g/12-oz. package ready-rolled puff pastry, chilled

about 200-g/7-oz. Brie, cut into 2-cm/³/₄-inch cubes

250 ml/1 cup cranberry sauce

fresh thyme sprigs, to garnish

a 24-hole non-stick mini muffin pan, lightly greased

MAKES 24

Preheat the oven to 200°C (400°F) Gas 6.

Use a sharp knife to cut the puff pastry sheet into 7.5-cm/3-inch squares. Press each square into the prepared muffin pan. Place a cube of Brie in each one and add about 2 teaspoons of cranberry sauce.

Bake in the preheated oven for 15–10 minutes until golden and puffed and the cheese has melted. Garnish with a sprig of thyme and serve warm.

CLOUDBERRY JAM GRILLED CHEESE

Vasterbotten is a popular Swedish cheese and cloudberry jam a Scandi favourite, with a tangy sour-sweet flavour. Combine them to make a mini grilled cheese. (Pictured page 76.)

85 g/3 oz. full-fat cream cheese
10 medium-thickness white
    bread slices
about 2 tablespoons cloudberry
    jam/jelly (available from
    specialist Scandinavian grocers,
    such as ScandiKitchen)
200 g/7 oz. Vasterbotten cheese,
    or a strong/sharp Cheddar
scissored chives, to finish
cocktail picks, to serve (optional)
a large baking sheet, lined with
    baking parchment

MAKES 20

Preheat the oven to 200°C (400°F) Gas 6.

Spread the cream cheese onto both sides of each slice of bread. Spread the jam/jelly thinly onto one side of the bread. Sprinkle half the grated cheese over 5 slices of bread. Firmly press the remaining bread slices on top to make sandwiches.

Place them on the prepared baking sheet. Sprinkle the remaining cheese across the top of the sandwiches. Bake for about about 10 minutes, until the cheese is golden and melted.

Sprinkle with chives, let cool slightly, then cut off the crusts with a serrated knife. Cut each sandwich into 4 small squares thread 2 or 3 of these onto a cocktail pick, if using. Serve warm.

POLENTA CUPS

175 g/³/₄ cup plus 1 teaspoon butter

175 g/³/₄ cup cream cheese

280 g/2 cups plus 2 tablespoons
plain/all-purpose flour

175 g/1¹/₈ cups polenta/cornmeal

a pinch of sea salt crystals

BLACK BEAN CHILLI

500 g/1 lb. 2 oz. dried black beans,
soaked in water overnight

2 teaspoons cumin seeds

2 teaspoons coriander seeds

2–3 tablespoons olive oil

4 shallots, finely chopped

3 garlic cloves, crushed

1 fresh green chilli/chile, chopped

1 fresh red chilli/chile, chopped

1 teaspoon soft brown sugar

2 teaspoons sea salt

50 g/2 oz. dark/bittersweet chocolate, grated

1 tablespoon tomato purée/paste

1 tablespoon freshly chopped coriander/cilantro

400 ml/1³/₄ cups crème fraiche/sour cream

smoked paprika, to sprinkle

4 or 5 x 12-hole mini muffin pans

MAKES ABOUT 60

Black Bean Chilli in Polenta Cups with Crème Fraîche

This canapé is useful as the cups and chilli can be made in advance. (Pictured opposite with a Paloma, see recipe page 63.)

Preheat the oven to 180°C (350°F) Gas 4.

First make the cups. Cream the butter and cream cheese together. Combine the flour, polenta/cornmeal and salt and add to the butter and cream cheese gradually, until the mixture forms a dough. Break off 3-cm/1¹/₄-in. balls and neatly press into the mini muffin pans, forming a cup shape. Bake in the preheated oven for 20 minutes until golden.

To make the chilli, put the drained black beans in a saucepan of fresh cold water, bring to the boil and cook for 1–1¹/₂ hours until tender. In a separate saucepan warm the spice seeds until just starting to pop, then remove from the pan and set aside. Gently heat the olive oil in the same pan and add the shallots, garlic and chillies/chiles. After 5 minutes add the sugar, salt, chocolate and tomato purée/paste. Cook for a further couple of minutes. Remove from the heat and let cool slightly, then blend in a food processor with the spice seeds. Combine with the black beans and fresh coriander/cilantro in a large bowl. Spoon into the cups, top with crème fraîche/sour cream and sprinkle over a little paprika.

Pink Grapefruit Ceviche-style Shrimp Skewers

finely grated zest and juice of 1 pink grapefruit

freshly squeezed juice of 2 limes

4 tablespoons light olive oil

1 fresh red chilli/chile, deseeded and
finely chopped

¹/₂ teaspoon salt

20 tiger prawns/shrimps, cooked and peeled

1 tablespoon chopped coriander/cilantro

1 spring onion/scallion, finely sliced

cocktail picks, to serve

MAKES 20

Here a simple citrus marinade gives cooked prawn/shrimp a pleasingly tangy taste. (Pictured page 67.)

Put the grapefruit zest and juice, lime juice, oil, chilli/chile and salt in a non-reactive bowl. Add the tiger prawns/shrimp, cover and chill in the fridge for 3 hours.

Put the chopped coriander/cilantro and spring onion/scallion in a bowl. Remove the prawns/shrimp from the marinade and toss them in the herb and onion to coat. Thread a prawn/shrimp onto each cocktail pick to serve.

PICKLED FIGS

400 ml/1³/₄ cups rosé wine

100 ml/7 tablespoons sweet raspberry
  vinegar

1 small fresh red chilli/chile

1 clove

6 dried lavender heads

250 g/9 oz. soft dried figs (about 10),
  quartered

LEMON BUFFALO MOZZARELLA

2–3 tablespoons extra virgin olive oil

grated zest and freshly squeezed juice
  of 1 small unwaxed lemon

1 teaspoon sea salt crystals

250 g/9 oz. buffalo mozzarella (about 2 balls)

CROSTINI

1–2 French sticks, each cut into
  1-cm/¹/₂-in. slices

MAKES ABOUT 20

LEMON BUFFALO MOZZARELLA & PICKLED FIGS ON CROSTINI

Only use the best buffalo mozzarella for this. This topping also works well on toasted ciabatta. (Pictured opposite.)

To make the pickled figs, put all the ingredients except the figs in a saucepan and reduce the liquid by half over a medium heat. Remove from the heat, add the figs and allow to cool.

For the mozzarella, pour the olive oil into a bowl and mix with the lemon zest and juice and the salt crystals. Tear the mozzarella in half and in half again, repeating until you have enough pieces to match your fig quarters. If the mozzarella is very soft, tear it in half, then cut it with scissors. Gently coat the mozzarella in the lemon mixture and leave for 1 hour to infuse.

Preheat the oven to 200°C (400°F) Gas 6. To make the crostini, bake the bread slices on baking sheets in the preheated oven for about 10–15 minutes until golden.

To assemble, put a piece of infused mozzarella and a pickled fig quarter on each crostini so they lean against each other. Serve immediately.

GREEN OLIVE & ANCHOVY TAPENADE ON CROSTINI

140 g/5 oz. good quality pitted green olives
  in Herbes de Provence

2 anchovy fillets (optional)

1 tablespoon capers, rinsed and drained

1 teaspoon lemon juice

1 small garlic clove

2 tablespoons extra-virgin olive oil

finely grated lemon zest, to garnish

freshly ground black pepper

MAKES 20 CROSTINI

This tangy tapenade spread on toast makes the ideal nibble. (Pictured page 10.)

To make the crostini, preheat the oven to 190°C (375°F) Gas 5.

Use a sharp bread knife to slice the frozen baguette as thinly as possible. Lay the slices out on a baking sheet and brush each one lightly with olive oil using a pastry brush. Turn and repeat. Place in the preheated oven and bake for about 10 minutes, until crisp and golden brown. Wait until they are cool before topping.

To make the tapenade, place all the ingredients in a food processor and purée until well combined and a spreadable paste in texture. Use a teaspoon to top each crostini with the tapenade, smooth slightly across the crostini with the back of a spoon, garnish with a pinch of finely grated lemon zest and a grinding of black pepper. Serve at room temperature.

CRAB FROMAGE FRAIS TOASTS
WITH CHIVE, CAPER & RADISH SALSA

1 slim baguette/French stick
500 g/1 lb. 2 oz. fresh crabmeat
200 g/1 cup fromage frais

CHIVE, CAPER & RADISH SALSA
200 g/7 oz. French breakfast radishes,
    roughly chopped
70 g/2½ oz. capers, drained and chopped
40 g/1½ oz. fresh chives, very finely
    snipped
4 tablespoons olive oil
4 tablespoons ginger wine

MAKES 40

Present a few of these toasts with the salsa on top as they look so pretty. You can serve the rest of the salsa in a bowl with a small serving spoon so your guests can add as much or little as they wish. (Pictured opposite.)

Preheat the oven to 200°C (400°F) Gas 6.
    Slice the French stick into 40 even slices and bake on baking sheets in the preheated oven for about 10 minutes, until nicely browned.
    Gently combine the fresh crabmeat and fromage frais in a bowl and chill. When you are ready to serve, mix all the salsa ingredients together in a separate bowl. Use a small palette knife to spread the cold crab mixture onto the toasts, then top with a little salsa. Serve immediately.

PEPPERED BEEF, WITH BLACKBERRY SAUCE
& WATERCRESS TOASTS

1 ciabatta loaf
400 g/14 oz. peppered roast beef slices
1 tablespoon olive oil
a handful of watercress

BLACKBERRY SAUCE
1 tablespoon balsamic vinegar
150 ml/⅔ cup beef or vegetable stock
2 tablespoons redcurrant jelly
1 small garlic clove, crushed
85 g/3 oz. frozen blackberries

MAKES ABOUT 20

A substantial bite, deliciously peppery and moreish. (Pictured on page 17.)

Preheat the oven to 200°C (400°F) Gas 6. To make the blackberry sauce, add the vinegar to a pan, pour in the stock and add the redcurrant jelly and garlic.
    Stir over a high heat to mix then add the blackberries and cook until softened. Mash them with a fork and stir. Set the sauce aside to cool. Cut the ciabatta loaf in half lengthways and toast under a hot grill/broiler for about 10 minutes until lighted toasted. Using a serrated bread knife, cut the bread on a diagonal into 5-cm/2-inch diamonds. Tear the beef into bite-size slices and place a few on each toast. Drizzle with the cooled blackberry sauce. Finish each one with a few sprigs of watercress.

FILLET STEAK ON TOAST WITH MUSTARD & ROCKET

1 ciabatta loaf
2 tablespoons wholegrain mustard
2 tablespoons mayonnaise
400 g/1 lb. beef fillet
1 tablespoon olive oil
50 g/2 oz. rocket/arugula
sea salt and cracked black pepper, to serve
a griddle pan

MAKES ABOUT 20

A satisfying combination of rare, juicy beef with mustard and peppery rocket/arugula. If you prefer, Dijon, English or honey mustard can be substituted for wholegrain mustard.

Preheat the oven to 200°C (400°F) Gas 6.

Cut the ciabatta loaf in half lengthways and toast in the preheated oven for about 10 minutes. Mix the mustard and mayonnaise together and spread evenly onto the cut halves of toasted ciabatta.

Brush the beef with the olive oil and heat a griddle pan. Sear the beef in the hot pan without disturbing, for about 2 minutes, and repeat on the other side. Transfer the beef to a chopping board and rest for 15 minutes.

Using a sharp knife, slice the beef into enough thin slices to cover the ciabatta. Press the beef gently onto the ciabatta, to encourage it to stick to the mustard mixture. Scatter the rocket/arugula over the beef and carefully cut into fingers. Serve with little dishes of sea salt and cracked black pepper.

PRAWN COCKTAIL SHOTS

200 g/scant 1 cup crème fraîche or sour cream
2 tablespoons tomato ketchup
2 teaspoons Manzanilla sherry
15 g/$\frac{1}{2}$ oz. each fresh tarragon leaves
    and fresh dill, chopped
1 teaspoon smoked paprika
a pinch of celery salt
15 g/$\frac{1}{2}$ oz. spring onions/scallions,
    chopped (optional)
400–500 g/14 oz.–1 lb. 2 oz. cooked and
    peeled king prawn/jumbo shrimps
    (about 60), tails left on if liked
1 tablespoon snipped fresh chives or a pinch
    of smoked paprika, to garnish
shot glasses or small tumblers
cocktail picks

MAKES 30

These miniature prawn/shrimp cocktails are eye-catching and popular, and an up-to-date version of a 70s classic. You will will need small shot glasses and good-looking cocktail sticks/toothpicks.

To make the cocktail sauce, put the crème fraîche, ketchup, sherry, herbs, paprika and celery salt in a small bowl. Mix with a fork or small whisk until well combined and smooth.

Spoon a little cocktail sauce into each shot glass and add a few chopped spring onions/scallions, if using. Thread 2 prawns/shrimp onto each cocktail stick/toothpick. Dip the prawns/shrimp into the remaining cocktail sauce, ensuring that they are coated, then carefully slide each stick into a shot glass, being careful not to smear sauce on the inside of the glass.

Garnish with either a sprinkling of chives or a pinch of smoked paprika, as preferred. Serve immediately.

GRILLED LAMB SKEWERS
WITH GARLIC & SAFFRON CUSTARD

The wonderful garlic and saffron sauce has the consistency of custard, but doesn't actually contain eggs. If the custard becomes too thick, dilute it with a little lemon juice or white wine.

500 g/1 lb. 2 oz. lamb loin fillet,
    cut into 30 cubes
2 tablespoons olive oil
1 tablespoon freshly chopped oregano
freshly ground black pepper

GARLIC & SAFFRON CUSTARD
50 g/3¹/₂ tablespoons butter
8–10 garlic cloves, coarsely grated
¹/₂ teaspoon saffron strands
500 ml/2 cups double/heavy cream
grated zest and freshly squeezed juice
    of 1 small unwaxed lemon
sea salt, to taste
30 wooden skewers, about 15 cm/6 in. long,
    soaked in water for 30 minutes before use

MAKES 30

Marinate the lamb in the olive oil, oregano and black pepper for about 2 hours.

When you are ready to cook, preheat the grill/broiler to medium.

Thread the lamb cubes onto the prepared wooden skewers and put them on a baking sheet, loosely covering the sticks with foil to prevent them from scorching. Set aside.

To make the custard, gently heat the butter, garlic and saffron together in a large, heavy-based frying pan/skillet. Add half the double/heavy cream and simmer until the cream bubbles and thickens, then add the lemon juice and turn down the heat.

Grill/broil the lamb skewers for 2–3 minutes on each side and keep warm until ready to serve.

Add the remaining cream, the lemon zest and salt to the saffron cream mixture and stir over low heat until you have a custard-like sauce. Pour into a bowl and serve with the aromatic lamb skewers.

STICKY DATES WITH LEMON FETA & WALNUTS

These canapés are refreshing, zesty and perfect with cocktails. Put the finished dates in the freezer for 5 minutes before serving as this somehow intensifies their honeyed sweetness. For meat lovers or those with nut allergies, chorizo is a great substitute for the walnuts.

200 g/7 oz. Greek feta cheese
grated zest of 1 unwaxed lemon and
    freshly squeezed juice of ¹/₂
20 Medjool dates, halved and stoned
100 g/3¹/₂ oz, walnut halves or diced
    chorizo sausage
sea salt and freshly ground black pepper
fresh mint leaves, to serve

MAKES 40

Cut the feta into 40 little blocks or mash it, as preferred. Put in a bowl with the lemon zest and juice and add salt to taste. Let stand for 30 minutes, turning occasionally.

Put a block or a small amount of mashed feta at one end of each date half, then add a walnut half (or chorizo piece, if using) to overlap the cheese. Grind a little black pepper over the top and finish with a mint leaf just before serving.

Pitta chips, eggplant caviar, mint & pomegranate

A deliciously light and velvety dip made from roasted aubergine/ eggplant makes the perfect topping. (Pictured page 75.)

EGGPLANT CAVIAR
2 medium aubergines/eggplants
1 garlic clove, crushed
freshly squeezed juice of $\frac{1}{2}$ lemon
2 tablespoons extra-virgin olive oil
1 tablespoon thick, Greek-style
    yogurt
salt and freshly ground
    black pepper
chopped fresh mint, to garnish
pomegranate seeds, to garnish
sumac, to garnish (optional)

PITTA CHIPS
2 pitta breads
sunflower oil, to grease
a lightly greased baking sheet

MAKES 20

To make the pitta chips, preheat the oven to 180°C (350°F) Gas 4.

Slice each pitta in half through the centre so it separates into two pieces. Cut both these pieces in half lengthways and then use scissors to snip each of these four pieces into eight triangles.

Arrange these on the prepared baking sheet, cook in the preheated oven for 10 minutes until crisp, then leave to cool. (Leftovers can be stored in an airtight container for 4–5 days.)

For the caviar, prick the aubergine/eggplant several times with a fork. Grill/broil it until the skin is black and blistered and the flesh feels soft. When cool enough to handle, peel off the charred skin. Place in a colander. Use your hands to squeeze out as much moisture as possible from the flesh.

Place the flesh, garlic, lemon juice, oil and yogurt in a food processor or blender. Pulse to a smooth purée. And salt and pepper to taste. Let cool completely.

Spoon a teaspoonful onto each baked pitta chip, sprinkle with fresh mint and a few pomegranate seeds and a pinch of sumac (if using).

CHEESE & SPICY ROASTED PINEAPPLE STICKS

Update the classic oh-so-retro 1970s pineapple and cheese cocktail nibble by charring the pineapple and rolling it in crunchy sesame seeds and hot red chilli/pepper flakes. (Also pictured on page 66.)

CHEESE & SPICY ROASTED PINEAPPLE STICKS
500 g/18 oz. fresh pineapple cubes
3 tablespoons toasted sesame seeds
¼ teaspoon chilli/hot red pepper flakes (finely ground in a mortar with a pestle)
a handful of fresh mint leaves, very finely chopped
250 g/9 oz. mild Cheddar or Monterey Jack, cut into 1-cm/½-inch cubes
cocktail picks, to serve

MAKES ABOUT 25

Preheat the oven to 180°C (350°F) Gas 4.

Put the pineapple cubes into a roasting pan and cook in the preheated oven for 35–40 minutes until golden then cover and set aside to cool.

Mix the sesame seeds, chilli/hot red pepper flakes and chopped mint in a bowl. Add the pineapple chunks and toss to coat. Thread the pineapple onto cocktail picks with a cube of cheese and serve.

Smoked Haddock & Celeriac on Pumpernickel with Beetroot Relish

This is a colourful and unusual canapé. As an alternative to smoked haddock, you could also use smoked mackerel or cod. For vegetarians, you could use slices of hard-boiled/cooked egg.

BEETROOT RELISH
200 g/7 oz. cooked beetroot/beets, finely diced
1 large shallot, finely chopped
1 tablespoon snipped fresh chives
2 tablespoons tomato purée/paste

SMOKED HADDOCK & CELERIAC
300 g/10½ oz. smoked mackerel fillet
200 g/7 oz. celeriac/celery root peeled
3 tablespoons good-quality mayonnaise
1 tablespoon horseradish sauce
500 g/1 lb. 2 oz. pumpernickel
fresh coriander/cilantro leaves, to garnish
    (optional)
a 5-cm/2-in. plain cookie cutter (optional)

MAKES 30–40

To make the relish, put all the ingredients in a bowl and mix to combine. Cover and refrigerate until needed.

Put the smoked haddock in a saucepan with just enough cold water to cover. Bring to the boil, reduce the heat and let simmer for about 2 minutes until cooked, then drain and flake (removing any skin and little bones). Leave to cool.

Coarsely grate the celeriac/celery root or shred it in a food processor. Transfer to a bowl and stir in the mayonnaise, horseradish and flaked haddock.

Cut the pumpernickel into 30–40 rounds using a 5-cm/2-in. plain cookie cutter or cut into squares, if preferred. Spoon a little haddock and celeriac/celery root mixture onto each one. Using a clean spoon, pile a little beetroot/beet relish on top and garnish with a coriander/cilantro leaf, if using, to finish. Serve at once.

Butternut Squash Hot Shots

3 tablespoons olive oil
1 onion, chopped
5 garlic cloves, crushed
1 fresh red chilli/chile, deseeded and chopped
1 teaspoon ras el hanout or mild curry powder
1 kg/2 lb. 4 oz. butternut squash, peeled, deseeded and chopped into chunks
1 litre/4 cups vegetable stock
100 g/3½ oz. sun-blush tomatoes in olive oil, drained
300 ml/1¼ cups fresh apple juice
300 ml/1¼ cups sour cream
sea salt and freshly ground black pepper
heatrproof shot glasses

MAKES 40–50 SHOTS

Offer friends a warm welcome on cold, dark nights with these little soup shots, warm in colour, taste and temperature.

Heat the olive oil in a large, heavy-based saucepan and gently fry the onion, garlic, chilli/chile and ras el hanout for a couple of minutes. Add the squash and fry for a further 5 minutes. Pour in the stock and cook for 10–12 minutes until the squash is tender. Remove from the heat and set aside to cool. Transfer the cooled squash to a food processor and add the tomatoes, apple juice and half the sour cream. Blend until very smooth. Season to taste.

When you are ready to serve, reheat the soup and use the remaining sour cream to bring it to drinking consistency. Try one before serving; if the soup is too thick it will stay in the glass so add a little more cream or water to thin it further.

Devilled Quail's Eggs

Quail's eggs always look so dainty and are the perfect size for canapés.
This recipe can easily be scaled up for a party and the eggs can be
cooked ahead of time. (Pictured page 108.)

6 quail's eggs
1 teaspoon mayonnaise
¼ teaspoon Dijon mustard
a dash of Tabasco sauce, or to taste
sweet smoked Spanish paprika
    (pimentòn dulce), to dust
a few pinches of smoked
    sea salt flakes
a few chives, snipped

MAKES 12

Rinse the eggs under warm water. Place in a saucepan and cover with cold water. Bring to a boil and cook for 4 minutes. Drain, rinse under cold running water, peel and pat dry.

Cut each egg in half lengthwise. Gently scoop out the yolks with a very small coffee spoon and put them into a bowl. Add the mayonnaise, mustard and Tabasco and mash. Fill the hollows in the whites with the yolk mixture. Dust with paprika, add a pinch of smoked salt flakes and serve with the chives scattered over.

Sesame Maple Turkey Fingers

The maple syrup will only subtly flavour the turkey, so offer more in a bowl as a dipping sauce. If you're entertaining children, omit the chilli and garlic from the recipe and they will love the turkey fingers.

4 tablespoons maple syrup, plus
   3 tablespoons extra for dipping
1 small red fresh chilli/chile, halved
   deseeded and finely chopped
1 teaspoon sea salt
1 garlic clove, crushed
500 g/18 oz. lean turkey breast
100 g/4 oz. sesame seeds, lightly
   toasted
fresh mint leaves, to scatter
baking sheets

MAKES ABOUT 40

Put the maple syrup, half the chilli/chile, the salt and garlic in a bowl and leave for 30 minutes.

Preheat the oven to 200°C (400°F) Gas 6. Cut the turkey breast into strips (about 40 in total). Coat the turkey fingers with the maple syrup mixture, then with the sesame seeds. Arrange slightly apart on baking sheets and cook for about 8 minutes, until cooked through.

Put the remaining chilli/chile and 3 tablespoons maple syrup in a small bowl as a dipping sauce. Scatter the mint leaves over the turkey and serve.

COCONUT & CARDAMOM CHICKEN

500 g/1 lb. 2 oz. skinless, boneless
    chicken breast, cubed
300 g/10½ oz. coconut cream
2 garlic cloves, crushed
1 small fresh red chilli/chile, deseeded
    and chopped
30 g/1 oz. fresh ginger, peeled and finely grated
1 star anise
seeds from 20 cardamom pods
2 teaspoons sea salt
2 tablespoons onion seeds, to serve
20 g/⅗ oz. fresh coriander/cilantro,
    chopped, to serve
6 long skewers, soaked in water for
    30 minutes before use if wooden
baking sheet
cocktail picks

MAKES 30–40

The coconut cream tenderizes the chicken, making it creamy and light, while cardamom adds an aromatic edge. It takes a little time to collect the cardamom seeds; use a rolling pin to crush the pods. These are luscious eaten hot or cold, so you could make them in advance, too. (Pictured opposite.)

Mix everything, except the salt, together in a bowl. Let marinate in the fridge for a few hours or overnight.

When you are ready to cook, preheat the oven to 200°C (400°F) Gas 6.

Add the salt to the chicken pieces and toss to mix, then thread them onto skewers. Arrange them in a single layer on a baking sheet. If you are using wooden skewers, cover them loosely with foil to prevent them from scorching. Cook in the preheated oven for about 10 minutes until the chicken is cooked through.

Remove the chicken from the skewers, scatter with the onion seeds and coriander/cilantro. Serve on cocktail sticks/toothpicks.

PANEER, MANGO CHUTNEY & CASHEW POPPADOMS

1 x 75-g/2½-oz. bag plain mini poppadoms
    (from the snack aisle in your supermarket)
2 tablespoons mango chutney
    (remove any large chunks of mango)
1 tablespoon apple cider vinegar
½ teaspoon mild curry powder
2 tablespoons mayonnaise
2 tablespoons plain/natural yogurt
150 g/5¼ oz. paneer (Indian cheese),
    cut into ½-cm/¼-inch cubes
50 g/2 oz. cashew nuts, roughly chopped
salt and freshly ground black pepper
2 teaspoons dry toasted nigella seeds,
    to garnish
fresh coriander/cilantro leaves, shredded,
    to garnish

MAKES ABOUT 20

Poppadoms are delicious dunked into mango chutney, hence the idea for using snack-size ones as a canapé base. Topped here with curried paneer cheese, they offer the perfect balance of crunch and creaminess, perfect paired with the Coconut & Cardamom Chicken (see above) and any gin and tonic.

To make the dressing, combine the chutney, vinegar, curry powder, mayonnaise and yogurt and season to taste. Add a few cubes of cheese to each poppadom and top with a teaspoonful of the dressing. Add a sprinkling of chopped cashews, coriander/cilantro and a few nigella seeds to garnish. Serve at once.

MINI CHERRY COCONUT MACAROONS

Macaroons, as opposed to French macarons, should be moist with sticky coconut. A lighter alternative to mince pies, enjoy these dunked in a hot toddy. (Pictured opposite with Cinnamon Buttered Rum, recipe page 104.)

4 x medium UK/large US
    egg whites
100 g/¹/₂ cup white caster/
    granulated sugar
1 teaspoon pure vanilla extract
¹/₄ teaspoon fine salt
200 g/3 cups sweetened
    desiccated/shredded coconut
about 20 undyed (natural colour)
    glace/candied cherries,
    very finely chopped
melted dark/bittersweet chocolate,
    to decorate (optional)
a large baking sheet, lined with
    baking parchment

MAKES ABOUT 24

Preheat the oven to 175°C (350°F) Gas 4.

Whisk the egg whites, sugar, vanilla and salt in a large bowl until the mixture is frothy. Add the coconut and chopped cherries and stir until combined.

Using wet hands work the mixture into small balls about 3-cm/1¹/₄-inches in diameter. Space them about 2.5 cm/1 inch or so apart on the baking sheet.

Bake in the preheated oven for about 10–20 minutes, until golden brown. Let cool on the baking sheet then transfer to a wire rack to cool. Drizzle with melted chocolate, if liked, and leave to set before serving.

Snowy Pine Nut Cookies

200 g/³/₄ cup plus 2 tablespoons butter, softened
100 g/¹/₂ cup plus 1 tablespoon caster/granulated sugar
200 g/1¹/₂ cups plain/all-purpose flour
¹/₂ teaspoon salt
200 g/1¹/₂ cups pine nuts, roughly chopped
1 teaspoon almond extract
icing/confectioner's sugar, for dredging

MAKES ABOUT 20

Rich, buttery and addictive! Serve this little sweet treats after savoury canapés. Ideal with sherry or dessert wine.

Preheat the oven to 180°C (350°F) Gas 4.

Put the butter and caster/granulated sugar in a bowl and beat until soft. Add the flour, salt, pine nuts and almond extract and mix well to combine. Using your hands, form the mixture into small balls about 4 cm/1¹/₂ in. in diameter. Place them slightly apart on baking sheets. Bake in the preheated oven for 12–15 minutes. Leave to cool a little before transferring to a wire rack and dredging with icing/confectioner's sugar. Dredge again when the cookies are cold and you are ready to serve them.

Apple & Calvados Pies

PASTRY
250 g/1³/₄ cups plus 2 tablespoons plain/all-purpose flour, plus extra for dusting
125 g/¹/₂ cup plus 1 tablespoon chilled butter, cut into cubes
75 g/¹/₂ cup plus ¹/₂ tablespoon icing/confectioner's sugar
1 egg
seeds from ¹/₂ vanilla pod/bean
1 tablespoon Calvados (French apple brandy)
fresh walnut halves, to decorate (optional)
milk, to glaze
icing/confectioner's sugar, for dredging

FILLING
100 ml/¹/₃ cup Calvados (apple brandy)
750 g/1 lb. 10 oz. eating apples, peeled, cored and finely chopped or roughly grated
150 g/³/₄ cup muscovado/dark brown sugar
75 g/¹/₃ cup butter
seeds from ¹/₂ vanilla pod/bean
6-cm/2¹/₂ in. and 5-cm/2-in. plain cookie cutters
2 x 12-hole mini muffin pans

MAKES 24

These are delicious served with gooey cheeses or with a big bowl of whipped cream. You can introduce a little variation by replacing some of the lids with a fresh walnut half.

Put the flour, butter and icing/confectioner's sugar in a food processor. Process until the mixture resembles fine breadcrumbs. Mix the egg with the vanilla seeds and Calvados and add to the mixture. Process quickly until it forms a lump of dough. Wrap the pastry in clingfilm/plastic wrap and chill in the fridge for 30 minutes. Meanwhile Preheat the oven to 200°C (400°F) Gas 6.

Put the apples in a bowl and splash the Calvados over the top. Leave to stand for 10 minutes. Put the apples in a heavy-based saucepan with the muscovado sugar, butter and vanilla seeds and set over medium heat. Cook until the apples are tender and the liquid has evaporated, stirring occasionally.

Lightly flour a work surface. Roll out the pastry carefully. You might have to do this in two batches. Stamp out 24 rounds using a 6-cm/2¹/₂-in. cutter and use them to line the mini muffin pans. Using a teaspoon, fill the pies with the apple filling; pack them quite full, but do not heap. Stamp out the remaining pastry using a 5-cm/2-in. cutter and press lightly onto the pies. Brush sparingly with milk. Bake in the preheated oven for 20–25 minutes. Cool on a wire rack and dredge with icing/confectioner's sugar to serve.

Salted Chocolate-Dipped Dried Figs

Dust a chocolate-dipped fig dusted with sparkling salt flakes and you have an indulgent treat for the legions of salted caramel devotees out there. Serve these as elegant (and easy to prepare) petit fours. (Pictured opposite with a Brandy Alexander, recipe page 107.)

100-g/3½-oz. bar 70% cocoa solids
    dark/bittersweet chocolate,
    snapped into pieces
12 small semi-soft ready-to-eat
    dried figs
sea salt flakes
a flat plate or tray lined with
    baking parchment

MAKES 12

Melt the chocolate in a heatproof bowl set over a pan of barely simmering water. Ensure that the base of the bowl does not touch the surface. Stir with a rubber spatula until melted.

Use your hands to massage the dried figs and shape them into their natural teardrop shape. Dip the base of each one into the melted chocolate and lay on it on the tray. Sprinkle sparingly with sea salt flakes and leave to set before serving.

INDEX

CREDITS

RECIPE CREDITS

Julia Charles
Apple Pie Moonshine
Aviation
Bee's Knees
Beetroot rosti with
    horseradish cream
    & dill
Blackberry Bellini
Bramble
Brandy Alexander
Brie & cranberry sauce
    puffs
Chambles
Cheese & spicy roasted
    pineapple sticks
Chelsea Sidecar
Chocatini
Cinnamon Buttered Rum
Clementine Caipirinha
Cloudberry jam grilled
    cheese
Crunchy crab salsa in
    cucumber boats
Cranberry & Orange
    Sparkler
Devilled quail's eggs
Endive cups with
    Roquefort mousse,
    pear & candied
    walnuts
Espresso Martini
Fireside Sangria
Goats' cheese & pink
    peppercorn balls
Green olive & anchovy
    tapenade on crostini
Home-made mini
    oatcakes with
    honey-roast salmon
    flakes & ginger butter
Kir Blush
La Paloma
Lavender French 75
Maple-roasted squash
    & whipped ricotta
    bruschetta with sage
Mini cherry coconut
    macaroons
Mini Margaritas
Mini Martinis

Moscow Mule
Old Fashioned
Paneer, mango chutney &
    cashew poppadoms
Parsnip & apple
    remoulade with
    bayonne ham on rye
Peppered beef with
    blackberry sauce &
    watercress toasts
Pink grapefruit ceviche-
    style shrimp skewers
Pisco Sour
Pitta chips, eggplant
    caviar, mint &
    pomegranate
Rose & Pomegranate
    Cosmo
Rusty Nail
Salted chocolate-dipped
    dried figs
Singapore Sling
Smoked salmon mousse
    croustades
Spicy Mexican corn
    & queso fresca
    quesadilla wedges
Spicy salt lime chicken
Swedish glögg
Vanilla White Lady

Jesse Estes
Black Manhattan
Bobby Burns
Brooklyn
Irish Coffee
Irish Flip
New York Sour
Sweet Manhattan
Vieux Carré
Ward Eight
White Manhattan

Lydia France
Anchovy wafers
Apple & Calvados pies
Black bean chilli in
    polenta cups with
    crème fraîche
Butternut squash hot
    shots
Caesar salad tartlets
Coconut & cardamom
    chicken
Crab fromage frais toasts
    with chive, caper &

radish salsa
Fillet steak on toast with
    mustard & rocket
Flash-seared tuna on rye
    with horseradish &
    tarragon cream
Grilled lamb skewers with
    garlic & saffron custard
Hot crumbed shrimp
    with tomato aïoli
Lemon buffalo
    mozzarella & pickled
    figs on crostini
Parmesan & sweet
    paprika biscuits
Prawn cocktail shots
Sesame maple turkey
    fingers
Slow-roasted tomato
    galettes with black
    olive tapenade &
    goats' cheese
Smoked haddock &
    celeriac on
    pumpernickel with
    beetroot relish
Snowy pine nut cookies
Spanish men
Sticky dates with lemon
    feta & walnuts
Vermouth scallops with
    green olive tapenade

Laura Gladwin
Appleblack
Bello Marcello
Bridge of Sighs
Cherry Baby
Cranberry Cassis
Festive Fizz
Havana Nights
Hibiscus Fizz
Kir Reali
Mimosa
Night Owl
Prima Donna
Prosecco Classico
Prosecco Cosmopolitan
Prosecco White Lady
Santa's Little Helper
Stiletto
Sparkling Manhattan
Zaza

Hannah Miles
Cheese straws

Ben Reed
Almond Martini
Black Russian
French 75
White Russian

**David T. Smith
& Keli Rivers**
Boulevardier
Kingston Negroni
Negroni Royale
Old Pal
Snowgroni

David T. Smith
Christmas Gin & Tonic
New Years' Eve Gin &
    Tonic
Winter Gin & Tonic